Birth of an Industry

Computers in the Early Years

Productivity Publications
Rochester, NY

Birth of an Industry

Computers in the Early Years

By Gene Denk

Productivity Publications
Rochester, NY

Table of Contents

Foreword
By Wilson Cooper

Gene Denk and I shared an office trailer across the street from the Navy's busy main runway at Point Mugu, California, in the early 1960s. His memoirs bring back many memories of those days when we rookie software developers were building the systems that were used to operate the Pacific Missile Range. The computers were huge in size, but their speeds were slow, their memories were tiny, and their operating systems were rudimentary.

Few of us had any training in computer science. Most systems were designed, written, tested, and cut over by small teams or by individuals. I don't recall a team of more than three people. Along the way, we immersed ourselves in the tools of the day that Gene describes in this book: SOS and SAP, SMASHT decks and binary patches, core dumps, and single-step troubleshooting.

Gene was an excellent developer, but I always thought his forte was troubleshooting the problems that arose at the hardware/software interface. He describes several of these: a missing bit in core memory, bad spots on magnetic tapes, and a misbehaving hydraulic actuator on a disk drive. I recall that he resolved many more issues.

Gene moves on from his days at Point Mugu and IBM to a sketch of how the Personal Computer emerged. Much of this material is new to me, and I have been delighted to read it.

Preface

I suppose it is natural for young people today to think that personal computers have been with us forever. Many adults know better, but how many knew the world of computers in the 1950s, '60s and '70s?

Perhaps you realize that there were no CDs back then, but can you imagine a computer without a disk drive? Without a monitor? Without an attached printer? Without a keyboard? Large-scale computers in the 1950s, which each cost millions of dollars and filled a space the size of a house, were missing all those features. A smart phone today has more power and connectivity.

In the late 1950s, having never even seen a computer, I was drawn to programming by a magnetism I could not resist. As a newcomer, I was in awe of the pioneers of the industry and, along with my peers, I learned the trade with little formal training. There was scant opportunity to get into the business except by reading what little was available and taking a great leap.

In this book, I will share the computer world as I knew it for the first few years after I joined it, because I feel those are the years most likely to be lost to posterity. Digital computers were in their infancy and the industry as a whole was new. It bore little resemblance to what we see today. The wonders of today's information age are the legacy of those early years.

Since my primary goal is to relate my experiences, I don't cover the entire industry. Although I share a few industry stories and history, much of the material deals with my own experiences, first as an employee of an IBM customer, and then as an IBM employee.

—Donald Eugene "Gene" Denk

Part 1: A Career in Computers

I am sure that our past determines, to a great extent, our future. What happened in our lives yesterday and what happens to us today prepares us for tomorrow. That has certainly been the case for me.

My boyhood informally taught me some mechanical skills. The U.S. Air Force gave me a foundation in electronics. College steered me into computers. I did not know it at the time, but these and other happenings in my life prepared me for my career.

Part I of this book will focus on my development in the computing industry and on advances in computer technology to create a context for Parts II and III, which go into detail about the evolution of computer technology from its early days through the advent of the PC. The way of life in the computer world at that time is a story that few people are left to tell, and it is important that those days are not forgotten. They were the foundation for the technology of today.

Chapter 1: The Path to my Future

My Young Life

I was born in 1932 during the Great Depression, shortly before my dad's service station led him into bankruptcy. I was the youngest of three children, so money was short in my childhood, but we were never short of love or discipline. Although we were taught the law of the clean plate, we never went hungry.

Mother was a registered nurse, a homemaker, and a good cook. She taught us about God, morality, and domestic skills. Dad was, at various times, a mechanic, a carpenter, and an outstanding machinist. Some of each rubbed off onto me.

In school I was an average student, getting top grades in the subjects that I liked, and mediocre grades in certain others, simply from a lack of willpower.

During my senior year at St. Vincent's High School in Vallejo, California, I joined the military. It happened somewhat by chance. Arriving at school one morning, two of my classmates were getting passes from the school office for an excused absence. It was March 1951, during the Korean Conflict, and those of us who were eighteen years of age were already registered for potential military draft upon graduation. My two classmates were preparing to leave for Travis Air Force Base, 25 miles distant, to join the Air Force Reserve. Seven of us boys went to Travis that day. We all joined the 1901st Airways and Air Communications Services (AACS) Squadron and became weekend warriors once a month. We each were selected to be trained either as a Radio Operator or a Radio Mechanic, Ground Equipment. I was to become a radio mechanic (now called an electronics technician). Three months later, we graduated from high school. We began two years' active duty the following month, on July 23. I went through an eight-month training course at Scott AFB, Illinois.

3

Our mission was to keep the ground-based communications equipment running, such as that found in control towers, direction finders, and instrument landing systems. My Air Force experience gave me a foundation in electronic hardware, a major key to my niche in the computer industry.

When I left high school, I had no intention of ever going to college, but by the time I left active military duty, I had applied to the all-male University of Santa Clara (later to become the coed Santa Clara University), to major in Electrical Engineering.

Over half of my freshman class consisted of veterans, recently separated from active military duty. That fact became known too late to the group of sophomores—only a year out of high school—who took it upon themselves to initiate us freshmen. One might say the initiation turned upside down.

I was not a good money manager in those years. Despite help from the GI Bill, my living and college expenses caused me to drop out of college for over a year while I worked in an oil refinery as a semi-skilled laborer to get my finances back into the black. I worked alongside men nearing retirement age and soon decided that I did not want to be in their position at their age, working with heavy, dangerous equipment on rotating shifts, outside, in all kinds of weather.

If my Air Force enlistment motivated me to start college, the oil refinery job motivated me to finish. I found a much less expensive school with great credentials: the California State Polytechnic College ("Cal Poly," now California Polytechnic State University) in San Luis Obispo, California. I was accepted with a major in Electronic Engineering.

The name San Luis Obispo will pop up in several places in this book. The mission, and later the town and the county, were named for St. Louis, the Bishop of Toulouse, France, by Franciscan missionaries in 1772.

I had over a dozen different jobs in my high school and college years, during school vacations, and sometimes during the school year. Some jobs involved driving trucks including, eventually, 18-wheelers during the summer of 1957 for Charles Jones Trucking based in Paso Robles, California (30 miles north of San Luis Obispo).

Charlie told me he had four daughters, only one of whom was married. I said I was a confirmed bachelor, focused on college. Little did I know that I would soon be smitten by his daughter, Lorraine. We married that December during my Christmas vacation from college, and we are still married today. I was 25 years of age and she was 23.

To be a Programmer

By 1957 I had fallen in love with computer programming, but I worried about making the wrong decision about a career change. Because of my six-year investment in electronics, it took me another year to make the decision to switch to computer programming. Agreement on a curriculum was still several years distant, and my faculty advisor had suggested that Mathematics was the best major for an aspiring programmer, so I finally switched my major to Mathematics. The term "Computer Science" did not become popular until three or four years after I graduated. Several illustrious proponents of Computer Science curricula published their recommendations in the *Journal of the Association for Computing Machinery*, "*Datamation*," and other trade publications. Standard Computer Science curricula took a few more years to gel.

While still an electronic engineering major at Cal Poly, I had taken every course the college offered dealing with digital devices. You could count them on the fingers of one hand, even if you were missing a couple fingers.

I remember Professor James Culbertson's course, Mathematics and Logic for Digital Devices. As a by-product of our studies, our class proofread and corrected the first edition of his new textbook of the same name. I still have it. He was a down-to-earth and patient teacher and was also a consultant for Librascope, a specialized computer manufacturer in southern California.

Another memorable course was Computer Programming, using the first textbook by Daniel McCracken, who was to become the famous author of several more programming language texts. To broaden his students' exposure to features, McCracken created an imaginary computer using a mixture of features of several real computers. He named it TYDAC, for *TYpical Digital Automatic Computer*. Names of several digital computers in the 1950s ended in AC, such as ENIAC, and EDVAC. For students such as us, who had no access to a real computer, his book was ideal.

For the programming course, our homework assignments were small programs of fifty lines or less in machine language. We even had to assign hardware addresses ourselves. There was no computer for us to use. If there was a digital computer within many miles, we were not aware of it (and the cost of using it would have been prohibitive). There were only a few computer installations in the entire state of California.

Each day, one of us would copy his program onto the chalkboard (white boards did not exist yet), and the class as a whole would visually search it for bugs.

I fared well in these sessions, because Lorraine usually helped me find some bugs the night before. I blessed her for doing that, since hunting for bugs was definitely not one of her favorite activities. Helping me during that course was all the programming she ever did.

At that time, the Electronic Engineering Department was building a power supply for a small computer that they hoped to build. Large commercially-built computers sold for millions of dollars each and used thousands of vacuum tubes. Transistors had been invented a decade earlier, but they were just beginning to replace vacuum tubes in the market.

In 1959 I selected the subject of machine assistance in coding for my Senior Project. I focused on an assembler program, SOAP II for the IBM 650 computer, and touched on the FORTRAN compiler. The IBM 650 was a medium-scale computer that was built by International Business Machines Corporation (IBM). In size it would fill a typical bedroom.

The other part of my senior project was about the FORmula TRANslator (FORTRAN), one of the world's first compiler languages. It had been invented in the mid-1950s and the compiler developed about 1957 at IBM. I entitled my project "Faster Coding for the Digital Computer."

I cited approximately two dozen books and commercial reference manuals—virtually everything I could find on the subject in libraries on and off campus and through scant industry contacts. It was challenging to find out what was being done commercially. It was difficult for outsiders to discover the existence of technical manuals for commercial products, and the manuals themselves were even harder to find.

Job Hunting

When I was about to graduate, I had interviews on campus with nearly a dozen potential employers. It was 10 months before Dwight D. Eisenhower would leave office as President of the United States of America, and the economy was in a recession. By the time my final exams were over, the list had been pruned to three job sites where I had scheduled visits:

1. Bendix Computers in Los Angeles,
2. Headquarters of the Pacific Missile Range (PMR) at Point Mugu (an hour north of Los Angeles), and
3. Edwards Air Force Base, where prototype military aircraft were tested (and still are) in the Mojave Desert of California.

Bendix manufactured a "small" computer, the G-15, which filled a set of cabinets assembled into a large L-shaped desk. The interview went poorly, so I was down to two potential employers.

Several months after my interview, the Bendix Computer Division was acquired by Control Data Corporation, a computer manufacturer which competed in the early 1960s with International Business Machines Corporation (IBM), Burroughs, General Electric, Honeywell, National Cash Register, Univac, and Radio Corporation of America (RCA). These companies were represented in the latter 1950s by the nickname "Snow White and the Seven Dwarfs," as coined by *Datamation Magazine*. IBM was Snow White. Other companies, such as Digital Equipment Corporation (1957), came along later.

I was offered Civil Service jobs that were attractive to me at Point Mugu and at Edwards.

The PMR job paid less. It was an entry-level GS-5a position at $4040 per year with no guaranteed promotions, but I had a chance to be on the ground floor to convert their operations to computers. The Edwards job would not be available for about three months. I had a wife and two small children to feed, so I took the lower-paying job at Point Mugu with the prospect of overtime to make up some of the difference.

I graduated at the end of the winter college quarter in March 1960 with a Bachelor of Science degree in Mathematics. Lorraine and I had two children by then: Charles (18 months) and Catherine (4 months). She was awarded a PHT, Pushing Hubby Through.

Chapter 2: The Pacific Missile Range

With my acceptance of the job offer at Point Mugu near the end of March 1960, I began a seven-year Civil Service stint with the U.S. Navy at Pacific Missile Range Headquarters.

Management Data Processing

I started out in the Management Data Processing Department (MDPD). That was a fancy name for the organization that did the data processing for payroll, cost accounting, supply, and various other management data functions.

I was taught how to use and program Electric Accounting Machines, but my assigned top priority was planning computer applications and to expedite acquisition of a computer. Most of my time was spent as a Tabulation Project Planner.

The MDPD job was well suited to my talents. I was in demand and I worked overtime during the week and nearly every Saturday, which helped us to make payments on some of our college debts. What time I had with my family was precious. I was promoted to GS-7a, with a sizable pay increase, after six months.

About that same time, I was asked to take a temporary assignment managing the office where all scheduled production jobs were audited for accuracy on their way into and out of MDPD. It was a quality control function. A team of three worked under me. Too many errors were being made in the very office that was responsible for catching errors in production jobs entering and leaving MDPD. Within a month we had reviewed our procedures, made changes where they were needed, and once again gained the confidence of the department and our users.

It was the first time I had ever managed a team. The three people on my team were opposites in several ways. I spent numerous sessions with my manager, getting his advice on dealing with personnel problems. The technical part of the job was easier than solving the personnel problems that had existed before I arrived and had indirectly caused the quality problems they were experiencing.

Shortly after that, a surprising opportunity jumped out at me, and I took it. I was only in MDPD for nine months, but I know I helped them significantly in that short time. That brief encounter with EAM was also to be of value to me in my later career.

Range Operations

The Range Operations Department was the scientific side of PMR. Range Operations' Test Data Division used contract personnel for all their (IBM 709) computer operations. In late 1960, I learned that they were going to phase out the contractor, replacing the contractor's people with Civil Service personnel. A few of the existing employees would join Civil Service, but most would be leaving. I applied and was their first hire. Talk about the ground floor! I transferred a half-mile down the street on the first work day of January 1961, with my ex-supervisors' sorrowful blessings.

With the Range Ops job, I converted to the Civil Service's promotion rules for professionals and soon got a multi-step promotion. In the first year, I wrote several applications programs and was borrowed by upper management to be a partner in a two-man task force for about three months to resolve a major information bottleneck. We succeeded (fortunately)!

One of our section heads (not mine) was unforgettable. He was brilliant on the job, but his personal life was a mess. More than once he arrived at work in the morning with a black eye or bruises from getting into a bar fight the night before. After a few months we didn't see him anymore. He was the first person I observed with that problem, but two others have passed through my life in the years since. In a way they remind me of something that President Calvin Coolidge said:

> "Nothing in the world can take the place of persistence.
> Talent will not; nothing is more common than unsuccessful men with talent.
> Genius will not; unrewarded genius is almost a proverb.
> Education will not; the world is full of educated derelicts.
> Persistence and determination alone are omnipotent.
> The slogan 'press on' has solved—and will always solve—the problems of the human race."

If I can lump *self-discipline* with persistence, maybe Mr. Coolidge's saying would apply to my three friends. My only problem with the saying is that Coolidge left God out of the last two lines.

In the early 1960s, the vast majority of the population had no concept of what computers were. One day Lorraine and I were at our doctor's office for an appointment. I looked at the sheet that the receptionist had filled out and given me to sign. On a previous visit I had listed my occupation as a Computer Programmer. The sheet that she gave me to sign said that I was a Computer. I did not even try to correct it.

In 1962, a man named Wilson Cooper, who had been the maintenance programmer for our locally-written operating system for a year or two, was promoted to be the technical manager of our Systems Programming Section. I was offered his prior position. I took it, working under him and with him. The technical aspects of some of our joint projects in the next three years are treated in Part II.

We had an unadvertised perk. We had knowledge of impending launches. At about "t minus two minutes," we could take a short break, go upstairs onto an observation deck, and watch a Nike-Zeus or some other missile streak into the sky from its launch pad.

The professional promotion feature of Civil Service provided for an automatic promotion to GS-9 after a year and a possible promotion after another year, based on merit, to GS-11. In 1964, with one year as a GS-11, I was eligible for promotion to GS-12. At that point in President Lyndon Johnson's term of office, all federal promotions were frozen for budgetary reasons. A few months later we learned that when one of our peers, whose promotion was pending but frozen, was offered higher pay by another prospective employer, his local promotion was magically and suddenly thawed out. Others decided to play the same game.

Several months later, I applied for an advertised GS-12 position at the Port Hueneme Naval Seabee base five miles up the coast from Point Mugu. I interviewed and was offered the job. When I told the PMR management of the offer, I got a quick promotion in time to thank the Port Hueneme folks and turn down the move. I was prepared to transfer to Port Hueneme if necessary, whereas some of my peers bluffed their way through.

In the mid-1960s as a GS-12, my gross pay was about $11,000. That was considered an enviable civil service wage, but the civil service pay scales were not keeping up with cost of living increases. By 1967 pay was significantly less than in private industry. Also, any potential advancement to GS-13 would have taken me completely away from programming and into full-time management. I did not want to do that. It was time to look elsewhere.

I sent resumes to some recruiters and interviewed with three companies on the east coast and one in the west.

My interviews at Bell Telephone Labs in Whippany, New Jersey, went well. I had two in the morning and one in the afternoon. I accepted the personnel chief's offer to take me to lunch. He put on his overcoat and asked me where mine was. I stated that an Air Force overcoat was the only one I had ever owned (having spent my life, except for the Air Force years, in the mild west coast climate). He thought I was joking and maybe still does. Later, I turned down their offer. I wanted more money than they were willing to pay.

My next interview was with General Electric in Valley Forge, Pennsylvania, for the Manned Orbiting Lab (MOL) project that was cancelled by Defense Secretary McNamara nine months later. Luckily, I turned that job down also.

My next interview was with IBM Federal Systems Division (space programs) in Gaithersburg, Maryland. That one had promise, but I still had one more interview on the west coast with IBM General Processing Division in San Jose, California.

My father, a retired machinist, had come to visit us just before I flew east for my three-day flurry of interviews. He understood employment offices, but he could not conceive of an agency that was paid by employers to go hunting for prospective employees and paying all costs at company expense. After I got back and was still on leave, Dad (72 years old at the time) helped me finish building a patio. I had started it three years before. We put our home up for sale and moved soon after. That was the first of three homes I fixed up just in time to sell and move.

Chapter 3: A Quarter Century with IBM

On Friday, June 2, 1967, I ended my Civil Service employment and on Monday, June 5, 1967, I went to work for the International Business Machines Corporation at its development laboratory and manufacturing plant three hundred miles north of Point Mugu in San Jose. IBM San Jose was mostly dedicated to developing and manufacturing magnetic disks and disk drives, an industry that, if not still in its infancy, was just a toddler, albeit a very lucrative one.

I took the job in the IBM San Jose plant for the type of work, location, and pay. About ten years later the guy from Personnel who had arranged my interviews and the follow-ups saw me and recognized me. He asked, in mock surprise with a twinkle in his eye, "Are you still here?" I imagine that encountering an employee he had processed into the company ten years before made him feel good. Moves were common in IBM, to the point where some people insisted, tongue-in-cheek, that the company initials stood for "I've Been Moved."

When I went to work in San Jose in 1967, IBM's mainframe computers were installed in what we called a "fish tank," so-called because the computer room was surrounded by windows. It was a showcase so tour groups could see what computers looked like. Only a small percentage of the population had ever seen a computer. The Navy's computers at Point Mugu had always been secure and out of sight, except for one day a year when we had an open house on Armed Forces Day. Within a year or two, with the various American campus riots in the late '60s, IBM made their computers much more secure.

I split my IBM career into two major areas: Manufacturing Automation for nine years and Product Test for sixteen, after being misplaced for my first three months. That short stint is rather humorous, looking back.

My first assignment was as a group leader of several programmer trainees who were developing specifications in preparation to program the Accounts Payable subsystem of CMIS (Corporate Management Information System). This was not what I had interviewed to do, but I dutifully performed to the best of my ability, even making a business trip to upstate New York.

I kept my eyes open and an opening came about three months later in the next department, which was involved with online control of the production line. It was one of the departments where I had originally interviewed, the one I had initially selected, and where I had thought I would be working. I transferred fifty feet down the hall.

Months later, when I was conversing with my manager, he told me how I had been "misplaced" back in June. While he was on a business trip, his staff programmer had performed my interview. My file was merged with the files of other pending new hires. He and my original manager had each chosen half of us by the equivalent of flipping a coin. The coin had flipped the wrong way for me, but the short assignment as the technical manager of half a dozen programmer trainees enhanced my teaching and leadership skills.

This little vignette leads to another tongue-in-cheek definition of the acronym, IBM: "I've Been Misplaced" (which is generally not true).

Manufacturing Automation

After my three-month misadventure in 1967, I spent nine years at IBM's San Jose manufacturing plant and development laboratory, supporting and creating programs for *manufacturing automation*. When people asked me what that meant, I would confuse them all the more by saying that we used computers to make computers (and peripheral devices, such as disk drives). We used computers and devices connected to them to produce and test components, subassemblies, and complete systems for sale around the world.

During those nine years from 1967 to 1976, in some ways the computer industry leapt forward and yet, in other ways, it remained in the Stone Age.

First of all, IBM's announcement of the System/360 family of computers in 1964 had forced every hardware or software vendor in the industry to take the same leap into the future or be buried. Several prominent computer manufacturers left the business. One of those was Radio Corporation of America (RCA), a diversified supplier of electronic products that chose to withdraw from the computer market because of the enormous new investment needed to remain competitive. IBM was still straining to catch up on backlogs to build and ship its computer hardware through most of the rest of that decade, a problem that many businesses only dream of having.

The new generation of (S/360) computers opened up opportunities for new applications. The people I worked with had previously created a network of over a hundred small satellite computers, each of which could communicate directly with an IBM 1460 mainframe computer, which would be known today as a server. At our earliest opportunity, we replaced the 1460 with twin S/360 Model 40s and added a teleprocessing network of over a hundred IBM 2260 video display terminals to automate communications with manufacturing workers.

In the same period of time, networking and teleprocessing gained a solid footing in the industry, at least among those companies near the leading edge of that technology, but I would say the really explosive growth came later, in the second half of the '70s and in the '80s.

Punched cards used for programs and data remained with us far too long, even with the advent of magnetic storage for the capture of keyed data.

Computer room procedures at IBM San Jose in 1973 were strikingly similar to those at the Pacific Missile Range in the 1960s. Although my company made teleprocessing terminals, the Information Systems group at IBM San Jose was not using them yet to make programming easier. Two reasons for that were the high cost of magnetic storage and resistance to change. Programs were still on punched cards. Turnaround time in the computer room for an assembly, compilation, or testing did not change much until we started to program online toward the mid-'70s.

For manufacturing plant floor automation, limits on random access memory (256K) in our computers precluded our use of compiler languages. Our online transaction processing programs were limited to 4K each, so they were all written in S/360 assembler language. The cost of memory had come down significantly, but it was still very expensive compared to today's costs.

The Product Test Lab Years

The next sixteen years of my time with IBM—1976 to 1992—were spent in the Product Test Laboratory: the first four years in San Jose and twelve years in Tucson, Arizona. The move to Tucson gave me a major promotion.

Market Changes

I think the most significant change in the industry during those sixteen years was the *miniaturization of electronic components,* including storage media. Around 1972 I remember a self-proclaimed manufacturing engineering "expert" saying that we had just about hit the limit for shrinking circuits and shortening cycle times. It reminds me of the story of the patent examiner who left that profession for another because "Just about everything worth inventing has been invented." The story ends by saying that the year was 1849. One basic fact in all of history is that those who say, "It can't be done," greatly outnumber those who go ahead and do it.

Automation has been a direct contributor to new technologies leading to progressive miniaturization, reduced production costs, and lower prices of products. As the price of a computer went from millions down to thousands of dollars, the market rose by similar orders of magnitude.

I noticed another byproduct of an enlarging market: *better software.* For example, choices of general-purpose database, query, and reporting systems in the years through the 1970s were very limited. None of the manufacturers went out of their way to be user-friendly because the market for software products was limited to a slowly-growing cadre of professionals on minis and mainframes. Because programs were targeted for professionals, interfaces did not have to be intuitive (no matter how much we wished they were). Limited sales generally equated to a limited development budget. The explosion in personal computer sales created a corresponding increase in the software market, leading to greatly increased development capital, improved price-performance, and user-friendliness because of increased competition in the larger market.

One example of user-driven demand affected the IBM PC. If people changed the hardware configuration of a PC in the early '80s, they would often learn—the hard way—that they had neglected to also flip one or more *dip switches,* tiny switches buried inside the computer case. Buyers hoped, requested, and demanded that the operating system be programmed to sense and adjust to hardware changes automatically. Their cries were heard, and suppliers slowly invested the time and money to make changes that would better accommodate their customers. Finally, there were no dip switches.

Management

I probably had close to a dozen managers during my time at IBM. That would be an average of a manager about every two years. Even considering my three transfers, managers tended to rotate every couple years to "broaden their perspective" for potential higher-level management positions. In that quarter century, I had only two managers who, I felt, should not have been in management.

I thought one of those two neglected his duties. He was finally forced to resign. The other tried so hard that he micro-managed a capable staff. One of my peers became so stressed that it caused medical problems that required a doctor's care. He healed after his transfer to another department. Another (junior) programmer would get so irritated at that same manager that he wanted to transfer. He came to me, unofficially, one day and told me he liked his job, but our manager was "driving him crazy." I shared his feelings, but I knew that amateur counselors can be dangerous.

I finally suggested, "We will probably have a new manager in a few months. If you can hang on, this too will pass."

He stayed, and in three months our manager became our ex-manager in a new (non-management) position that fit him well, and we had yet another new manager to orient into our tiny sector of the business.

In general, my managers throughout my career were excellent. I had a female manager for a couple years, and we got along just fine. I had two managers who were outstanding. One was soon promoted to second-level management.

Someone had quipped before my transfer to the Test Lab, "Most people who go to Product Test don't ever leave." It proved to be true for me. I was attached to the Product Test Laboratory until I retired on my sixtieth birthday in October 1992.

Chapter 4: Retirement

When I turned fifty—ten years before I was expected to retire—IBM sent Lorraine and me to a week-long seminar on retirement. We gained a lot of knowledge and important guidelines. During the first hour our instructor asked us to write down the answer to a single question: "What is it that you intend to do when you retire?"

One of the most common answers was, "Clean out the garage."

"How long will that take you?" was the next question.

The point our teacher was making was that we should have long-term goals that would keep us occupied indefinitely. Those who sit and watch television all day tend to atrophy and die early.

The teacher told us that retired men tend to stay in the house excessively and become "efficiency experts," observing and advising their wives on how they should do various chores which the wives had each already done thousands of times over the decades. At that point, many of the wives had smirks on their faces.

Over the next nine years at work, I pondered the "what will I do?" question and developed some answers. Those answers are different for each of us. Note that I said, "nine" years. Before my formal retirement, I spent a year and a quarter on a leave of absence, free of my past career, but without a paycheck.

One new phenomenon at IBM starting in the mid-1980s was the buy-out, which numerous companies used to reduce head counts. A company would offer their older, higher-paid employees a handsome lump sum payment in return for their departure. The company would reduce head count for payroll savings over the longer term.

I eventually took a buyout in July 1991, receiving a large lump sum. I chose to take a fifteen-month leave of absence, delaying my retirement until October 1992 to avoid a reduction in my monthly pension. That particular buyout was the first one at

IBM that did not exclude programmers as "critical resources." It coincided with our empty nest at home. Our youngest daughter, Joanne, had recently graduated from high school and beauty school and had ventured out into the permanent workforce.

Obsolescence

On the day after my regular IBM employment ended, I was obsolete. Perhaps that's stretching the point, but there is some truth in it. Friends had advised me to become a consultant. I told them it was time for me to do something that didn't require 12-to-14-hour days. In a high-tech job, one must spend significant time learning new things online, in formal classes, or from trade publications. I looked back through my career and estimated that I had spent an average of five weeks a year—10% of my time—in classes, not counting my informal education.

Short Second Career

One of my life's ambitions was to run my own business. I studied business opportunities, and in August 1992 (two months before my official IBM retirement), Lorraine and I opened our Postal Connection store in Tucson. We had fourteen departments or business units.

We kept one PC at home, one in the store, and had a computerized parcel system. I would have been lost without the computers as tools to run the business. We both waited on customers. In our spare time, Lorraine was the personnel department and I was the accounting department. I did the accounts receivable/payable, cash flow, payroll, inventory, and accounting, all on a laptop computer and a printer on my desk. Twenty years earlier, that amount of computing power would have occupied a very large room in a commercial building. The cost would have bankrupted us in one day.

We were in business for three years ("only 10–12 hours a day" for me), and then we retired again. We both learned many valuable lessons and facts of life while we were in business. We left with many cherished memories and few regrets.

Real Retirement

My next goal in life was to be a "full timer" in the parlance of recreational vehicle owners. Lorraine's and my possessions shrunk dramatically (like computers had). Our home in Tucson sat on a half-acre lot, with 3000 square feet under the roof, a pool, and a spa. Our volunteer labor force had all left and it was much more than we needed or cared to maintain by ourselves.

We moved into our 33-foot motorhome, sold or donated most of our belongings, put the rest in storage, and sold our home.

The divestiture took some discipline. If we hadn't used something in a year and didn't have a solid prediction about needing it, out it went! We gave our collections away to those who would care for them. Lorraine's collection of several hundred salt and pepper shakers went to our daughter Cathy and her mate. My 485 unique Boy Scout mugs (which had filled floor-to-ceiling racks on both sides of the foyer wall in our house) went to the Otis H. Chidester Scout Museum of Southern Arizona in Tucson.

Did we miss what we had divested? No. We had many good memories and a new adventure in our lives. If we are lucky, we will know when it is time to let go of anything.

Our first month-long pause "on the road" was in Gresham (Portland), Oregon for our son Joe's wedding to Elisa Bardi.

Our kids made sure we had a cell phone. It was a three-watt "bag phone" (the size of a thousand-page book) that I could connect to a whip antenna high up on the motor home. There was hardly a place, even in the "boondocks," where we could not transmit to a cell tower.

We often stopped to cook and eat at rest stops along the highway. One evening, while Lorraine was cooking, I phoned several of our West Coast kids' homes and found them all at one house, celebrating the July birthdays. "Where are you?" they asked.

"We're cooking dinner in a rest stop on I-25, just north of Wheatland, Wyoming," I replied. I switched on the speaker, and we had a nice, if fairly short, conversation.

I say "fairly short" because we paid thirty-nine cents for every minute on the air. That was in 1996. The cell phone business was just starting to grow rapidly. Now cell phones can take photos and surf the internet. In 1996, that wasn't even a dream!

We drifted through the western half of the U.S. for four years, pulling a car behind us. The car went many more miles on its own than behind the motor home, wherever we happened to be.

In spare time while we were on the road, I took a correspondence course to learn how to create back-of-the-book indexes. Indexing is a profession! I completed the course in about a year with the invaluable aid of a computer program named MACREX. Then I decided not to go into the business, even though I could have done so in the motor home. One ancillary thing I learned was that, before personal computers and indexing programs were available, indexes were created on—did you guess the answer?—index cards. Authors are discouraged from writing indexes for their own books because it is a specialized skill, but I did! (How well did I do?)

We had two laptop computers, "his and hers," that we used for hobbies, personal business, and later, volunteer work. I mostly used word processors, spreadsheets, and publishing programs. Lorraine's usage was slightly different. I sometimes kept a travel log and sent it to our sons and daughters at the end of a month of travels.

We returned to San Luis Obispo to stay in 1999 and now live a half-mile from our honeymoon home of a half century ago, a converted garage that we lived in for a while in 1958. At that time, a computer was a monstrous machine that few people had heard of, that fewer still had ever seen a picture of, and that an even smaller little-known group of pioneers had seen or touched in person.

From being a *programmer* in my profession, I have become just a computer *user*, acquiring already-written programs for every need I have. Once again, that phenomenon is a result of market size.

People with a personal computer problem always seem to turn first to a friend who is (or was) in the computer industry. Desiderius Erasmus of Rotterdam once said, "In the land of the blind, the one-eyed man is king."

Once in a while, when asked to solve someone's PC problem, I could and did. Most of the time I could not, and they were left to find another "one-eyed man" or pay a professional for his or her time, also paying the techie for the investment in a continuing education. Sometimes the person would buy a new computer when all their old one needed was a tune-up. The bottom line is that I have not even tried to keep up with the industry since I left it, simply because I have other ways to spend my time.

My grandmother and grandfather relied on real horse power on their farm back in the early 1900s. Then Grandma won a Model-T Ford—their first motor vehicle—in a raffle. Her teenagers, including my mother-to-be, quickly learned how to drive it, but Grandpa could never get the hang of it. It would not respond to "Gee" and "Haw" for him. He was lucky not to get killed driving it.

That is somewhat how I am with much of the new digital technology. I have no idea how to use my grandson's iPod. I may never graduate from penciling into my pocket datebook to a Personal Digital Assistant. A real advance for me was a cell phone that takes pictures and emails them, but I have no desire for one that plays movies. I understand digital TV, but my eyesight is such that changing to high definition TV hardly matters to me. At my age, I am a hunter, not a shopper. If I think I need something, I hunt for it, but I'm too busy with my volunteer life to go shopping for things I do not think I need. So, you see, I really am obsolete, and it does not bother me in the least that I am "over the hill."

I have been asked by several people what retirement is like. My best response is, "Retirement is when you can work harder doing what you want to do for free than you ever did in your career." I still put in some fourteen-hour workdays, but only if and when I want to.

My wife says, "I see him more than before, but I still don't have his attention. He's in his world, busy doing his thing." Writing this book is one example (but she really does know how to get my attention).

Part II: The Evolution of Digital Computers

There are two major types of computer: analog and digital. Analog means continuous, so an analog computer is one that operates on continuous measurements. A very simple example of an analog computer is the venerable old slide rule, made obsolete by digital calculators. This is not a book about analog computers; it is a book about digital computers. This is the only time that analog computers will be mentioned in this book. When "computer" is encountered from this point on, it will refer to a digital computer.

What did we use, other than pencil and paper, before computers?

Where did digital computers come from?

What were the characteristics of early computers and what was it like to program them?

How did we evolve from a world of mainframe computers to personal computers that are accessible to everyone?

I will try to answer these and other questions in the following chapters, along with telling many personal stories.

Chapter 5: The Invention of Computers

Early Pioneers

Who invented the digital computer?

It might have been the Chinese, who developed the abacus. I kept an abacus on my office shelf throughout my career, as a reminder of the time when mankind's tools were very basic. My abacus also came to mind sometimes when a power outage brought my electrical world to a halt.

Some people will tell you it was Blaise Pascal. He built a mechanical calculator named the *Arithmatique* in 1642. Each digit position was changed by a geared wheel. When a wheel turned one complete revolution (marked from 0 to 9), representing a power of ten, it would turn the next higher-order wheel one digit. Older vehicle odometers copied that technique.

A few people might say the inventor was Wilhelm Schikard, who created a machine that could add, subtract, multiply, and divide using sprocketed wheels, nineteen years before Pascal built his calculator.

Many say it was British scientist Charles Babbage, who invented his *Difference Engine* in the early 1820s and the *Analytical Engine*, a programmable mechanical calculator, in 1830. He worked for three decades—the rest of his life—for acceptance. It was in vain. His machines were ahead of their time, in that their many tiny gears each had to be hand-made and patiently trimmed to fit. The precision needed for mass production was not yet attainable, and he was unable to get the support he needed. The Difference Engine was never completed and construction of the Analytical Engine was never started.

Babbage's huge steam-powered Analytical Engine, had it ever been built, would have used punched cards for memory and could have printed its answers, somewhat similar in concept to its electrically-powered successors of the twentieth century.

Konrad Zuse's Z Series and the S1 Computer

In 1935 a young German engineer named Konrad Zuse agonized over the immensity of the task of solving simultaneous linear equations containing dozens of variables. With only (rooms full of) desk calculators and only human hands to write extensive intermediate results, he had the same basic problems that were frustrating two other pioneers, Howard Aiken and John Atanasoff, at about the same time. It is unlikely that any of the three knew about the work of the other two, especially Zuse, whose work was in secret, designing airplanes for Adolph Hitler's air force.

Zuse's frustrations were finally rewarded by his creativity in designing and building his first computer, the Z1, in 1938. It was *mechanical*. It was followed by the *electrical* Z2, which ran with used telephone relays. In 1941 he created the Z3. Zuse also produced the S1 special-purpose computer, which designed guidance systems for the Nazis' feared glider bombs, used effectively against allied shipping toward the end of the war. Finally, he produced the Z4 in the closing months of the war, too late for it to help the German war effort. None of Zuse's computers were electronic, partly due to a shortage of vacuum tubes.

Years after the 1945 end of World War II, the "secret" of Zuse's inventions became public knowledge. The Z3 is thought by some to have been the world's first fully automatic digital computer. However, it was not electronic; it was electric, using banks of relays. The most remarkable aspect of Zuse's computers was their small size. The Z3 was installed in a closet in Zuse's home. The S1 is said to have looked "like a coffin set on end." [1]

Automatic Sequence Controlled Calculator

Howard Aiken proposed his (relay-operated, therefore *electric*—not electronic) *Automatic Sequence Controlled Calculator* in 1937. After several frustrating rejections, Aiken finally built his Mark I in collaboration with IBM, the U.S. Navy, and Harvard University. It contained three-quarters of a million parts and was completed in 1944. According to IBM's archives, "Over 50 feet long, 8 feet high and weighing

---

1   David Ritchie, The Computer Pioneers (New York:Simon and Schuster, 1986), p. 66.

almost 5 tons, the Mark I took less than a second to solve an addition problem but about six seconds for multiplication and twice as long for division, far slower than any pocket calculator today."

Aiken went on to build Mark II, III, and IV. The latter two were *electronic*. He predicted that the United States would never need more than a half-dozen computers.

Alan Turing put his concept of a computing machine on paper in 1937, followed by more of his expositions for more than a decade. His *Turing Machine* eventually became a basic model of computer and program architecture. Turing is said to have been a key in producing the British *Bombe Machine* to break Germany's *Enigma code* during World War II, but it is possible that many of his contributions, however great, are still British war secrets.

None of the people mentioned above held a patent for the stored-program digital computer. That patent was held jointly by two men, Dr. John Mauchly and Dr. J. Presper Eckert, for twenty-seven years before it was declared invalid. Credit for the invention was shifted to others, notably Dr. John Atanasoff. The story that follows, in some ways, is stranger than fiction!

John Atanasoff

John Vincent Atanasoff, frustrated by the drudgery of solving many complex equations while working on his doctorate at the University of Wisconsin in 1929, tried and failed—at that time—to postulate an accurate automatic computer. Years later, while employed at Iowa State College in the 1930s, he again felt the urgent need for such a calculator to solve problems in theoretical mathematics. He agonized over the design of such a machine over a seven-year period.

Atanasoff's frustrations came to a head one cold winter evening in 1937. His mind was swimming in a myriad of confusing concepts. Frustrated, he rushed from his office, got into his car, and sped aimlessly for over 200 miles, going fast enough to have to concentrate on driving rather than on the ocean of conceptual details that had been plaguing him. Crossing the Mississippi River into the state of Illinois near Rock Island after midnight, he stopped at a tavern. There were none in the "dry" state of Iowa. Once relaxed, the most important concepts began to jell in his mind. By his account, he worked for three hours recording the design while in the roadhouse.

In my mind, I picture Dr. Atanasoff sitting alone at a table in a back corner, using napkins and anything else he could find to write on, jubilantly and furiously recording the key ideas that were finally clear in his mind, lest they escape after all those years of frustration. Many of us have gone through lesser versions of that experience.

Four basic principles sorted themselves out in Atanasoff's mind while he sat in the roadhouse:

1. The digital concept and the need to use the binary number system.[2]
2. The concept of serial calculation.
3. Basic memory design, using condensers (now known as capacitors) and refreshing their charges by a process called "jogging."
4. Basic design of logic circuitry.

Excited and happy with resolution of the basic design principles, he returned to Ames and amplified them on paper over the next days.

A year later in the fall of 1939, armed with a $650 grant, Atanasoff hired a bright graduate student named Clifford Berry and bought parts to build a prototype. They had the prototype in operation before Christmas. Because the prototype used vacuum tubes (for several purposes), it is considered by many to have been the first electronic digital computer.

In December 1940, work on the actual Atanasoff-Berry Computer (ABC) commenced. It would be able to solve large systems of simultaneous linear equations—thirty equations with thirty unknowns. It would fit on top of a large desk.

Atanasoff met Dr. John Mauchly, a physicist, at a scientific conference in Philadelphia. Mauchly also had an urgent need for an automatic computer and, over a period of time, he plied Atanasoff and Berry for information, which they did not withhold.

The United States was drawn into World War II in December 1941. In early 1942, because the ABC was not considered to be essential for the war effort, Atanasoff would soon go on to an unrelated wartime job with the Naval Ordinance Laboratory. Berry's new employer would be Consolidated Engineering Corporation in California. Mauchly's wartime job would lead to a new application of Atanasoff's ideas.

Work on the ABC was suspended; it was never completed. It is said to have been salvaged for parts, some years later, by a student who had no idea what it was.

At the time of his departure, Atanasoff thought he had prepared Iowa State College to obtain patent rights on the automatic electronic digital computer, but no

---

2   Norbert Wiener, in the early twentieth century, had postulated that just as humans invented decimal arithmetic because that is how many fingers we have, electronic devices are best suited to binary arithmetic because they best recognize only two states.

patent ever came from that effort. Perhaps those holding the budget purse strings felt it was a waste of time and money. Even decades later, many leaders in the computer industry vastly underestimated the potential of computers, so what would you expect from nontechnical administrators?

Presper Eckert and John Mauchly

In Mauchly's job at the Moore School, University of Pennsylvania, he and a graduate student, J. Presper Eckert, worked on complex mathematical computations defining ballistic trajectories for the Army. All the while, they shared a passion to automate such calculations, and certain features of the ABC design were fundamental to that desire.

ENIAC

In 1943 the climate was ripe, so to speak, for Mauchly, Eckert, and their associates to propose an "Electronic Diff. Analyzer" (sic) to the (Army's) Ballistic Research Laboratory. As a result of the Army's needs and a powerful presentation, they got the contract. Thus began development of a computer named ENIAC (Electronic Numerical Integrator And Computer).

Upon its completion in 1945, ENIAC was said to have accurately solved a test problem in an hour that had taken two person-years with desk calculators. ENIAC is thought to have been the first large electronic computer (versus computers based on relays and other electric devices). ENIAC used over 18,000 vacuum tubes, weighed about thirty tons, and required about 175 kilowatts of electricity to run. It used the decimal number system by configuring a string of ten vacuum tubes for each digit in each computational register. ENIAC was used extensively for development of postwar (cold war) weaponry, particularly atomic weapons, and eventually survived relocation to the Ballistic Research Lab in Aberdeen. ENIAC was in use for a total of ten years.

Through a series of questionable circumstances, Eckert and Mauchly bargained the patent rights away from the university after the war was over, resigned their positions at the university in 1946, and filed patent applications for ENIAC soon after.

EDVAC, EDSAC, and Other "ACs"

Eckert and Mauchly built the EDVAC (Electronic Discrete Variable Automatic Computer) in 1947–48 from John von Neumann's design. EDVAC is said by some to have been the first *stored-program* digital computer.

Others maintain that the EDSAC (Electronic Delay Storage Automatic Computer) was the first stored-program digital computer. An Englishman, Maurice Wilkes, attended a set of lectures about ENIAC at the Moore School in 1946. Wilkes also took a copy of von Neumann's design notes for what would become the EDVAC home with him to England. It is claimed that EDSAC was in operation before EDVAC.

There are those who maintain that the SEAC (Standards Eastern Automatic Computer) and the SWAC (Standards Western Automatic Computer) may have been the first stored-program digital computers. Built concurrently by the National Bureau of Standards, they are said to have been put to work just a few months before EDVAC. I wonder about that, since EDVAC was supposedly built in 1947–48, and SEAC and SWAC, supposedly, in 1950.

In all four of those computers, the advent of new storage technologies made the stored program concept feasible.Other descendants of the EDVAC architecture were the MANIAC, the JOHNNIAC (in honor of John von Neumann), and the ILLIAC.

In 1949 Mauchly and Eckert created BINAC (BINary Automatic Computer), the prototype for the commercial UNIVAC system.

UNIVAC

In 1950 the Eckert-Mauchly Computer Corporation needed to raise capital for commercial production. For that purpose, it was sold to Remington Rand and renamed Univac. Early in 1951, the first UNIVersal Automatic Computer was sold to the U.S. Census Bureau. In 1952 Remington Rand also bought Electronic Research Associates of St. Paul, Minnesota, which then collaborated with the Univac division to produce later models of the UNIVAC computer series. In 1955 Remington Rand was sold to the Sperry Corporation to become Sperry Rand.

UNIVAC was the first commercial stored-program digital computer, and for years the company exacted royalties from competing commercial computer manufacturers. UNIVAC contained about 5,000 vacuum tubes, took 100 kilowatts of power, occupied almost 1,000 cubic feet, and weighed about 8 tons. By 1957 there were 46 UNIVACs.

Invalid Patent

One of Univac's competitors, Honeywell, challenged the patent in 1967, refused to pay royalties, and was sued. They counter-sued. In the ensuing federal court case in Minneapolis, Honeywell presented a mountain of evidence.

It was from that courtroom that the computer world learned of Dr. John Vincent Atanasoff and his invention. The original of an early letter from Mauchly to Atanasoff shook the industry. It also became public knowledge at that time that ENIAC had been used to perform calculations for the hydrogen bomb, well over a year before the patent application. Under the weight of evidence, the patent was declared invalid in 1973.

Selective Sequence Electronic Calculator (SSEC)

In 1948 IBM created the SSEC, using 12,000 electronic vacuum tubes and 21,000 electric relays. It occupied a glassed show-space on the ground floor at IBM's headquarters in New York City. SSEC was certainly not state-of-the-art. Its time, however, was rented out to various agencies and businesses for $300 per hour. The SSEC was perhaps a good lesson for IBM's engineers of what not to do when it created its next computer.

Whirlwind

The Whirlwind started out to be the first flight simulator. It needed lots of memory. The projected memory requirements went far beyond what the current technology of mercury delay tubes or Williams tubes could provide. Whirlwind would be the first computer to use a memory type whose invention it necessitated: magnetic core memory. Whirlwind began its working life in 1951.

Even core memory fell far short of the continuously increasing requirements for simulations. At the same time, another critical defense need arose, to which Whirlwind was deployed for the next years instead.

The Defense Calculator (IBM 701)

With the advent of the Korean War in 1950, IBM was asked by the U.S. government to build a large scientific computer for help in the war effort. As a result, the IBM 701 Electronic Data Processing System, also known as the Defense Calculator, emerged in 1953. IBM built nineteen 701s, the first time that IBM had built more than one of the same model. It was less than a quarter the size of its immediate predecessor, the SSEC, and 25 times faster. The 701 was to become the patriarch of a decade's worth of computer systems: the 70x and 709x series. The 701s had electrostatic storage tube memories, and secondary magnetic drum storage.

The IBM 702

IBM also announced a commercial counterpart of the 701 in 1953: the IBM 702. It was a decimal machine, with a capacity of over 10,000 decimal characters in Williams tube memory—a bank of 84 cathode ray tubes upon whose faces could be stored those thousands of decimal characters (and accessed at the rate of 23 microseconds per character). The Williams tubes were to be replaced later with the more reliable magnetic core memory. The 702 ran fastest on magnetic tape input and output, though it could handle cards, albeit more slowly. It could perform ten million operations per hour. The 702 was replaced by the IBM 705 in a short period of time.

The IBM 650

Also in 1953, IBM announced its card-based medium-size *IBM 650 Magnetic Drum Data Processing Machine*, which was very different from IBM's other computers. The 650 was developed in a different IBM laboratory. The 650 was made to provide a migration path to computers for customers using the 600-series calculators[3] and associated Electric Accounting Machinery. IBM had expected to sell fifty 650s. During the late 1950s it had acquired the moniker "The workhorse of modern industry." By the time it was taken out of production in 1962, almost two thousand had been built, outselling any competitor or predecessor.

The IBM 704

In 1954 the IBM 704 Data Processing System succeeded the 701. An important new feature was its fully automated floating point arithmetic. It used magnetic core memory. The time to do an arithmetic operation was cut in half, down to 240 microseconds for multiplication or division and 84 microseconds for addition or subtraction. The 704 was the immediate predecessor of the IBM 709, which is the subject of an entire chapter.

The IBM 705

The IBM 705 replaced the 702 in 1954. It was architecturally similar to the 702, but far more advanced. As did the later 702s, it had magnetic core storage, but twice as much. Other improvements included more than a sixfold increase in instruction execution, a more powerful instruction set, and overlapping input and output operations.

In 1961 the 705 was replaced by the transistorized IBM 7080, which also had much more storage than the 705.

---

3   These calculators were as tall as a person. Refer to the IBM 604 in the next chapter.

Other IBM models

Besides the IBM computers named above, there were the 7040 and 7044 that could be directly coupled to the 7094 to handle its input and output. There were the 1401, 1410, and 1460 medium-scale computers and their mainframe counterpart, the 7010. There were the 7070, 7072, and 7074 (10-digit) decimal computers. Finally, there was the IBM 7030 Stretch supercomputer and certainly some other early IBM computers that I have missed.

A Heavy Burden

My object is not to exhaustively name every computer ever built by IBM, but to provide a context for the unusual time of early growth of the industry. The parade of new machines paralleled the growth of memory and input/output technologies.

There were over a half-dozen serious competitors, each churning out competing systems with different architectures and technologies, all incompatible with each other. The IBM System/360 (1964), eventually provided the basis for a long-term solution to that problem, but in the meantime, there were no standards! Everyone was experimenting. It made for difficult decisions and many technical issues.

A Look at Computer Memory

Digital computers are typically divided into a few basic components. John von Neumann defined them very effectively as:

- A central control (central processing) unit,
- An arithmetic unit,
- A memory unit,
- Input and output devices, and
- A recording device.

The greatest challenge in creating these early basic components was in the realm of memory devices.

Condenser Memory

Atanasoff struggled with tradeoffs between reliability and expense. Vacuum tubes were expensive, generated much heat, and consumed great amounts of power. He struggled with alternatives, finally conceiving of a scheme using inexpensive condensers (now we call them capacitors).

Each condenser, representing a binary bit, could be charged or not charged with a voltage to represent a 1 or a 0. The first problem with such a scheme was the fact that each condenser's charge would dissipate in a few moments. Atanasoff and Berry built a commutator—a round disk with 25 condensers[4] and 25 contacts mounted on each side—which would sequentially connect each condenser to a vacuum tube long enough to sense a charge in the condenser, thus reading that bit. If there were a charge, it would trigger the vacuum tube to regenerate the charge before connecting to the next condenser. Atanasoff called this process "jogging" (as in jogging a person's own memory). The commutator turned at one revolution per second.

Drum Memory

Atanasoff and Berry also created a secondary (slower) magnetic drum storage, but they did not invent it. That honor goes to Gustav Tauschek, an Austrian, in 1932 (the year I was born). A cylinder, or drum, was covered with a magnetic coating and read/write heads were mounted over the surface of the spinning drum to read or write data in tracks around the circumference.

Some computers have used drums for primary storage, but drums have mostly been used as a slower secondary storage. With the proliferation of semiconductor memory, magnetic drums became history.

Mercury Delay Tube Storage

Mercury delay storage is based on two basic principles of physics:

1. Vibrations at one end of a long, narrow pool of mercury will transmit through the pool, back and forth, until exhausted.
2. An electrically-charged piezoelectric quartz crystal transforms electrical charges into mechanical vibrations and vibrations into electrical charges.

---

4   Twenty-five condensers stored 25 binary bits, equivalent to an 8-digit decimal number.

A mercury delay tube memory was created by filling a tube several feet long with mercury, plugging both ends with quartz crystals, and attaching appropriate circuitry to each end. One tube could contain hundreds of bits. One crystal wrote binary bits into the tube of mercury. At the other end, the bits were read. A circuit for jogging completed the design.

A rack holding dozens of mercury delay tubes could replace an older memory many times larger in physical size. Storage cost was reduced by orders of magnitude. Conversely, the amount of storage could be radically increased. It made von Neumann's stored program concept feasible.

Mercury delay storage was replaced by core memory in the latter 1950s for reasons of cost and accuracy.

Williams Tube Memory

Williams-Kilburn tube memories were invented in England, at Manchester University by F.C. Williams and Thomas Kilburn. Their idea was to use a cathode ray tube's electron beam to place charges representing binary bits on a grid on the inside of the CRT's screen, which was about four or five inches square. Every few milliseconds, those bits would be read back and then recharged (or "jogged," if we were to re-use Atanasoff's terminology).

Magnetic Core Memory

Core memory, or simply core, as it became known, was the brainchild of Jay Forrester, who was a member of the team that built Whirlwind at MIT. It was responsible for a major leap forward in memory size and dependability.

Core memory was our high-speed random access memory. Today's solid-state replacement of core is known as RAM. Imagine a desktop containing a 1982 Personal Computer with about 128K or 256K of memory. Explode that desktop to be a room the size of a house and then, in your mind's eye, take the RAM out of the PC, and expand it from the palm of your hand into a large cabinet standing on the floor. The cabinet containing the core memory for IBM's 709x machines was about six feet long, six feet high, and held 32,768 words of 36 bits each, or 196,608 six-bit characters and was considered to be a large memory—the most available in the early 1960s.

Each binary bit—0 or 1—lived in a tiny ferrite-powder-saturated ceramic "doughnut" (called a ring or a core) less than a millimeter in diameter.

The rings were arranged in arrays, e.g. 128 by 256 (32,768 bits). All the rings in each horizontal row had an X wire strung through them. All the rings in each vertical column had a Y wire strung through them. Each intersection of X and Y represented a unique address. A third—diagonal—wire also ran through each ring as a sense/inhibit wire. One such array was called a *memory plane*, and 36 of those memory planes, addressed identically, made 32,768 36-bit words. Thus, one complete word could be accessed during each memory cycle.

An electrical current through a core generated a magnetic field. A field of sufficient magnitude would set the magnetic polarity of the core to north or south, depending on current direction. If half the current needed to change polarity was supplied on one X wire and half on one Y wire, the bit at their intersection—and only that bit in its plane—would change. Selected *sense/inhibit wires* could have a reverse current to inhibit the setting of corresponding bits in appropriate memory planes of a word. The same sense/inhibit wires were switched to a different function—sense—when it was time to read the bits. The operation was somewhat more complex, but the preceding explanation will suffice for the purpose of this book.

Magnetic core memory plane

Core memory was initially expensive (about $1 per bit), but it was very reliable. The cost of core memory dropped by orders of magnitude over the next years, making core memory the least expensive, most dependable memory until the advent of silicon memory chips in the later 1960s. In the early '70s when chips made of silica attained production status, old core memory planes became office decorations.

While memory was being updated and expanded in capacity, so were operating systems and input/output technologies. It was an exciting time of change, as systems moved from uniquely designed applications to mass-produced, standardized systems and from research and testing mode to full commercial application.

My own experiences mirrored the experiences of many others. In the chapters to come, I will explore the growth of the industry through the lens of my own experiences.

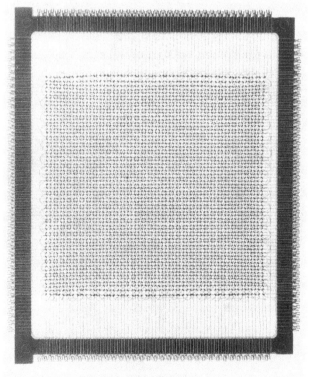

Magnetic core memory plane

Chapter 6: Practical Applications: Electric Accounting Machines

When I went to work for the Management Data Processing Department at Point Mugu, that accounting group did not have a computer. They were planning to have occasional access to the Range Operations Department's IBM 709, a large-scale "scientific" computer that occupied the entire wing of a building about a half-mile down the street from MDPD. I became one of a dozen people called Tabulation Project Planners, who figured out how to accomplish various accounting tasks on *Electric Accounting Machinery*. Looking back, I would say they were analogous to today's systems analysts and computer programmers (or software engineers, to use a more recent term), but they did it with pluggable wires instead of computer code.

Our job was to create or modify accounting jobs to be run on *Electric Accounting Machines* ("EAM"), a predecessor of digital computers, based on the processing of data in the form of punched cards.

Punched cards go back two centuries. In 1801 Joseph Marie Jacquard used them to program the automated loom that he invented.

The EAM industry was started by a man named Herman Hollerith over a century ago. When the U.S. government took almost ten years to manually process the 1890 Census, he found a way to do it in less than one-third the time. Hollerith devised a punched card where the locations of tiny holes defined numbers. To implement the card scheme, he devised rudimentary equipment for quickly punching, reading, and tabulating the census data in cards. The first EAM was born.

The keyword was *electric*, as opposed to *electronic*. A few of the tasks performed by computers today were done in the first half of the 20th century by a variety of machines: sorters, collators, interpreters, reproducing punches, and accounting machines. Those machines each had a different purpose, but each had a card reader and a card transport mechanism. They were controlled, or programmed, by pluggable wires connected to relays and other components through a control panel.

- The *sorter* was used to put a deck of punched cards into a desired sequence. There might be several thousand cards, one for each employee, to be sorted by employee number.
- The *collator* was used to merge two decks of cards. Both decks would have been pre-sorted on the data field they would be merged on. For example, a card containing employee hours worked might be merged behind the employee's master card (containing pay rate, etc.).
- The *interpreter* was used to print the contents of cards along their tops so that, when necessary, people could read them. Reading the tops of interpreted cards was much faster than visually scanning the holes.
- The *reproducing punch*, officially named *Document Originating Machine*, would copy the holes (data) in selected columns from each master card and punch that data into a corresponding data card that had been previously merged (behind its master card) on the collator. An example would be the employee's pay rate.
- The IBM 407 *accounting machine* could store a few dozen characters in memory, add or subtract numeric values in counters, print data from the cards in the form of a printed report, and optionally send information through a cable to a punch machine, creating a new deck of cards.

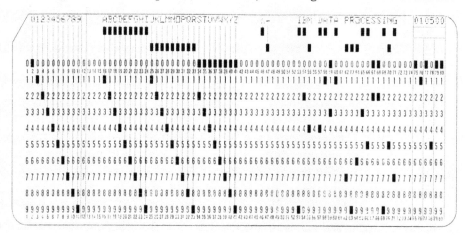

Hollerith card

We also had an IBM 604 Calculator, and it was partially *electronic*. For payroll, it could multiply the number of hours worked times hourly pay rate, calculate taxes, and punch the results into a data card.

The Tab Project Planner would analyze the requirements for a new job to be done periodically, such as a biweekly cost accounting, plan in detail each step to be done, and painstakingly write a very detailed procedure for machine operators to follow. EAM used wired-program removable control panels. Those for the sorter, collator, interpreter and reproducer were relatively simple and fairly standard. In general, a control panel for the IBM 407 accounting machine part of each periodic job was permanently and uniquely wired ("programmed") and could be quite complex. Each job would, typically, use its own uniquely-wired 407 control panel like the one pictured below. My observation is that the wiring of this panel is relatively light.

The IBM 407 Control Panel

IBM assigned a Customer Engineer to maintain the machines, all of which IBM leased to us. His job was to keep all those machines working properly. When the manuals did not have answers to my questions, I sometimes picked his brain on the inner workings of a machine and occasionally got it to do some unadvertised function for our benefit.

EAM was a lark for me. My combination of mechanical and electrical backgrounds allowed me to understand *how* the machines worked, not merely *what* they were meant to do.

My first week in MDPD was spent learning to operate and program the simpler machines. For the second week, I was sent to a weeklong Introductory IBM 407 Accounting Machine course at IBM's education center on Wilshire Boulevard in Los Angeles.

After about three months on the job, I wired a control panel for a project that my peers, some of whom had been there for years, said could not be done. I wired (programmed) the control panel so that the machine would remember more alphabetic data than it was designed to do. My boss cancelled my scheduled return to school for the advanced course, saying that I could probably teach it.

Not that I didn't get an occasional dose of humility! After wiring a control panel for a new job, we would next debug it (just as computer programmers do). Any wire in the wrong plug would cause a malfunction, which we would have to discover and fix. I was trying the "impossible" one day, and I got a result that turned dozens of eyes in that cavernous workroom. My IBM 407 accounting machine laced a card; that is, it punched all 960 possible holes. Starting in the top row, all eighty punch dies slammed through the card at the same instant, then repeated that eleven times. It sounded like a machine gun. It was over in a second. It even aroused my boss's attention on the inside of a glass-paned office. I took some good-natured ribbing over that one.

In the 1950s and 1960s, many EAM shops converted their data processing to commercially available digital computers. By the 1970s EAM shops were mostly unheard of anymore.

Before we describe the computers from the mid-'60s to the end of the 20th century, I feel a need to describe the computing environment, starting when I dove into it headfirst in 1961.

What were the more detailed characteristics of just one series of early computers and what was it like to program them? I will give my personal answers to those questions for the IBM 709 and its two successors in the next chapters.

Chapter 7: The IBM 709x Series Computers

My highest priority in the Management Data Processing Department was to help plan the conversion from EAM to a computer. In mid-1960 I went off to the IBM education center again, this time to take an IBM 709 Computer Programming course. The 709 was a large-scale computer that IBM first sold in 1957. I had previously acquired an IBM 709 Principles of Operations Manual and had nearly memorized some important parts of it.

Arriving at school the first morning, I found a room that said "IBM 709 Programming" on the door and sat down in the classroom. Preliminaries done, the instructor began teaching about I/O traps (that term would be more recognizable on later computers as I/O interrupts). Well, I was able to understand with somewhat of a struggle, but wondered if I was in the wrong class. At the first recess, I talked to the teacher and discovered I was in the Advanced 709 Programming class, whereupon I moved to the Introductory 709 Programming class on another floor, having missed their first hour or so.

Four months after that class, in the first week of 1961 my transfer to the Test Data Division of the Range Operations Department at Point Mugu took effect.

Baptism into the World of Computers

My branch manager-to-be was still an employee of the contractor during my first week. He would be officially hired into civil service a week later, followed by dozens of programmers and programmer trainees. In general, the colleges and universities that the graduates came from had few (if any) courses in computers or programming, so we would have to train them. Had it been five or ten years later, there would have been Computer Science curricula at most of the schools.

The Programming Branch would be organized into sections, each with a technical manager. The branch manager, who liked to be called by his nickname, Jim, would be our administrative manager.

After some preliminaries, my first real task was to write a glossary of computer terms. There were three existing publications that Jim or I could find with some of that information, and our new programmer trainees would need much more. In partnership with a technical writer, I produced the Glossary of Programming and Computing Terms. It had to be done rather quickly. We registered it with the Armed Services Technical Information Agency (ASTIA) and updated it two years later. The revised edition grew to fifty-five pages. After that, *Datamation* (a trade publication) and others filled the vacuum with glossaries that were far more comprehensive than ours.

As the first crop of programmers and programmer trainees were reporting in, and between my glossary activities, I helped with some of the logistics of preparing for an on-site IBM 709 programming course. Our IBM Systems Engineer arranged for an IBM programming teacher to be brought in. As I recall, the classroom was within a half mile of the Pacific Ocean, which was a big morale booster for some of our new trainees.

I started programming the IBM 709, a large-scale computer that occupied the entire wing of a building.

The IBM 709

The IBM 709 contained thousands of vacuum tubes. The filaments of several tubes were expected to burn out whenever power was turned on. The Customer Engineers would have to search out and replace the modules containing blown tubes before the system would be operable. As you may suspect, it was seldom powered off.

The IBM 709x series machines were octal. Its engineers and programmers used the base 8 number system. The computer, of course, was binary, but we represented its numbers with octal digits representing three binary bits each. This was in contrast to the hexadecimal (base 16) number system used for most of the later computers (including PCs).

Memory was organized in words of 36 bits each. Integers and floating point numbers were each, normally, a word in length.

The IBM 709 and its peripherals

Character Codes

Each character was represented by six bits in the Binary-Coded Decimal Interchange Code (BCDIC), commonly called BCD (pronounced by sounding the letters: "bee-cee-dee") and defining 47 characters including digits 0 to 9, the upper-case alphabet, and a few special characters. Lower case was not possible, so very little documentation was stored in the computer. Six of these characters could be contained in a word.

The bulk of our documentation was typed by technical writers and not stored on any media except paper because no electronic media was available yet. Our copies were made on a machine that used an ammonia process. Sometime around 1962, we got our first electrostatic copier from Xerox, at that time a little-known company. Xerography caused a worldwide office revolution. Previously, copies were always obviously copies. Suddenly, one could hardly tell the difference between the master and the copy.

It was in the early 1960s that the American National Standards Institute established a 7-bit character code standard and called it ASCII ("ask-ee") which was an acronym for American Standard Code for Information Interchange. It allowed for up to 128 unique combinations of binary bits, defining the ten decimal digits, the lowercase and uppercase alphabet, and between two and three dozen each of special characters and control characters. It could not be used, of course, in the 709x series computers.

In designing their next generation of computer systems (S/360) with 8-bit characters, announced in 1964, IBM allowed ASCII mode as a data option, but created a preferred 8-bit coding scheme called Extended Binary-Coded Decimal Interchange Code, known universally as EBCDIC (pronounced "ebb-see-dick"). EBCDIC contained 256 possible combinations of bits, by which all commonly-used characters and more could be represented. It became a de facto standard for many IBM customers.

Components

The 709 consisted of many boxes, or units. Most boxes were about three feet deep, three feet wide, give or take a foot, and about six feet tall, with some notable exceptions. The operator's console was a complex of lights and switches on the Central Processor Unit, with a desk-like shelf for the operator. When the 7090 came along, the operator's console was separated from the CPU.

The 709x series had no keyboard. One reason was that every second of time was precious on a computer worth millions of dollars. The rationale was that any input to the 709 should be prepared off-line on magnetic tape that could be read quickly.

The 709x could do only one task at a time, in serial fashion. Personal computers in the early 1980s were like that. The general introduction to multitasking on IBM computers started with the next generation of computers after the 709x series, S/360 in the mid-'60s.

The 709x did not have a display tube either. Messages from the operating system were output to the online printer. It printed rather slowly, on the order of 120 lines per minute. Early PC users might imagine that as slightly faster than one of the early dot-matrix printers. How could a system whose time was so valuable afford to wait for such a slow device? There were two answers:

1. Only cursory messages—one-liners in general—were sent to the online printer (as operator instructions), so an infrequent message would have finished printing by the time the computer operator took several steps to read it.
2. The IBM 716 online printer, to me, looked very similar to the printing part of the IBM 407 Accounting Machine, an inexpensive expedient, if true. High-speed printing of data was done off-line.

Our 709 read many thousands of punched card images each shift. It did not read information from the cards directly, but rather at a dramatically higher speed from magnetic tape, onto which their data had been copied, as 80-character records, by means of an off-line card-to-tape machine. Likewise, printer output from the 709 went to tape and then, off-line, to the printer. The 709x could not read input or print output in background mode because it could not multitask.

Around 1961, we acquired an IBM 1401 medium-scale computer. It had a high-speed card reader and a printer that printed 1200 lines per minute. The 1401 replaced the card-to-tape and tape-to-printer machines. Those tasks were its main justification. In other words, a medium-size computer with a fast card reader and a fast printer was cost-justified to serve a large-scale computer with neither of those capabilities. That complication would disappear with the next generation of computers.

Well over a dozen IBM 729 tape drives were connected to our 709. Magnetic tape was its lifeblood. Its only other input device was a very slow card reader, and its only other output was the slow online printer. One tape drive was dedicated to read the input streams of card images that had been copied to magnetic tapes off-line. Another drive was for the output destined to be printed. On another drive was a tape containing the operating system, of which only small parts would fit into high-speed memory at a particular moment. On another was a library of application programs. Other tape drives were used for data, such as input, transient data between serially-running programs, and output not destined to be printed.

Each 10½-inch reel could hold 2400 feet of tape—almost a half-mile. Each tape drive was about 3 ft. square and 5 or 6 ft. high, so just imagine how much space 18 drives took.

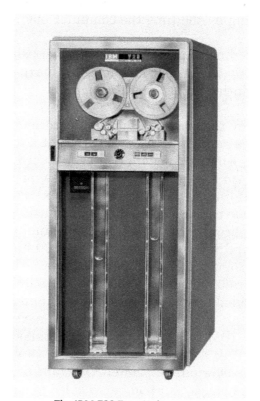

The IBM 729 Tape Unit

Heat Problems

A consequence of the 709, with all its vacuum tube filaments, was the vast air conditioning required to keep the computer room cool enough—below the maximum operating temperature for the system's most temperature-sensitive component, core memory. The air conditioning was designed with our prevailing breezes in mind—off the ocean and cool. About a half-dozen times a year, when the hot "Santa Ana" winds were blowing from the east, we would have to shut down for a day or two. Imagine bringing the busy Pacific Missile Range to a standstill for a day or so because the computers were too hot! We would typically get a thermal check in the core memory unit, which meant that our main memory had just shut itself down.

The IBM 7090 and 7094

In 1961 we replaced our 709 with a 7090, a transistorized replacement for the 709. The transistor had been invented in the 1940s. A tiny piece of silicon, treated with controlled impurities ("doped") would become a semiconductor and replace a vacuum tube. Control Data Corporation had put the first transistorized large-scale computer on the market in early 1958 and IBM followed suit early in 1959 with the 7090, the fastest computer in the world at that time.

When the 7090 replaced the 709, there were no longer several thousand vacuum tube filaments heating the computer room, so our temperature problems ended. Two years later, we got our first 7094, an upgrade from the 7090. Its main advantages to programmers were another increase in speed and seven index registers instead of three. I don't remember if it used circuit chips. They had been invented in 1959.

The 709/7090/7094 represented a sequence of technology rather than a family. They were all one size. They were upward compatible (with minor exceptions) because the 7090 and 7094 were *replacements*. The 7090 was a transistorized 709, and the 7094 applied more new technology to the 7090 architecture.

Computer Speeds

Today's computers—even personal computers and tablets—run at speeds in the GHz range.

The 709's cycle time of 12 microseconds would convert to a speed of 1/12 MHz.

The 7090's cycle time of 2.18 microseconds would be a speed of about half a MHz, or less than a thousandth as fast as some of the slower PCs today.

The 7094's cycle time was 1.4 microseconds, a speed of about 0.7 MHz.

Actually, today's units of measure for speed, GHz, MHz, or the more basic unit, Hertz, were not yet in use in the early 1960s. The equivalent of today's MHz was Mc (megacycles), or millions of cycles per second.

Punched Cards

In the early days, the only way we could originate data was through punched cards. Keyboards attached to computers came much later. We would write a program on paper, submit it to a roomful of keypunch operators, and work on other tasks while we were waiting for the punched card deck, usually at least overnight.

When we found a bug, we would often wait in line for the only keypunch we were allowed to use. We could punch only a few replacement cards ourselves. Think of a "10 Items or Less" line in a supermarket, and then think of a singular keypunch, with people often in line behind the current user.

We had hundreds of thousands of cards stored in some areas. We overloaded a wooden floor where we put several card files adjacent to each other in a temporary office trailer. We had several card file cabinets backed up to a room divider wall in the middle of the trailer. One day we discovered that there was an inch separation between the floor and the middle of the wall halfway across the trailer. The weight had pushed a concrete pier underneath the frame into the pavement.

When devices became available for recording directly onto tapes and later, disks, a growing body of industry leaders advocated the elimination of punched cards. There were also diehards who did not trust magnetic media and predicted data disasters if we did away with cards. It took another decade for cards to disappear. I still saw some card readers in 1980.

Patching Binary Cards

As a systems programmer, I could sometimes hasten the solution to a crisis by patching a binary card deck. It sometimes saved an hour or so of precious time as a temporary fix to one of my problems or someone else's.

It was fairly easy to unpunch a hole. I would lay the card on a hard surface and place a chad[1] in the selected hole. Then I would use my fingernail to iron it into place, flat and even but upside down so that its presence was visually more obvious. It would stay in place for at least one pass through a card reader. That was all we needed, pending a permanent fix.

It was more challenging to punch a hole where there was none before. With a razor blade I could do fairly well, if I exercised some patience. If there were many holes to cut, it would become too time-consuming.

---

1   We should all know what a chad is, after the November 2000 election in Florida. It is the little rectangular piece that is punched out.

IBM 010 Key Punch

Someone found an antique IBM 010 keypunch in a closet and I took possession of it. Very few of us were skilled in making patches to binary cards, and my circumstance was such that I made most of them. The 010 became a precious tool for me at such times. The 010 was an ancestor of the IBM 029 keypunch.

The 010 was the size of a large loaf of bread and sat on top of my filing cabinet. It had twelve punch keys, one for each of the twelve rows from the top to the bottom of the card. The twelve rows were named the 12-row, 11-row, 0-row, 1-row, and so on down to the 9-row. In binary cards, each punch represented a binary 1-bit.

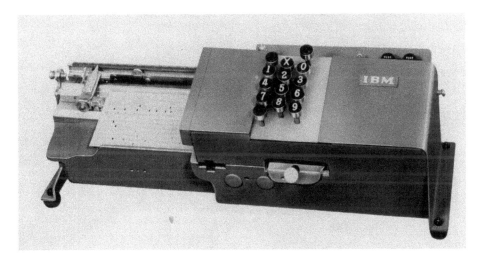

Type 010 key punch.

The twelve punch keys on the 010 keypunch machine were arranged in a matrix, three keys wide and four high. We thought in the octal number system. Each row of three keys represented an octal digit. When punching replacement cards, I learned to rest my fingers on the keypad, read octal from a paper and/or the old card, and punch by touch without looking at the keypad. It could be compared to using one of today's numeric keypads.

IBM 029 Key Punch

The 029 was integrated into a desk-like table and had an alphanumeric keyboard.

IBM 029 Key Punch

Column Binary Cards

We mostly worked with column binary cards, where 3 columns times 12 rows made 36 bits—one word—allowing 24 words to fit into 72 columns. Columns 73–80 usually contained an 8-character card sequence field in Hollerith code, so that the deck could be re-sorted in case it was accidentally dropped.

A column binary card is pictured in the figure below. Column numbers (1 to 80) are printed along the bottom of the card. The first two words (6 columns) were for system control and a checksum. Note the remaining 22_{10} word numbers in octal notation across the top. The 4s, 2s, and 1s in the main body of the card represented the octal values of those bit positions.

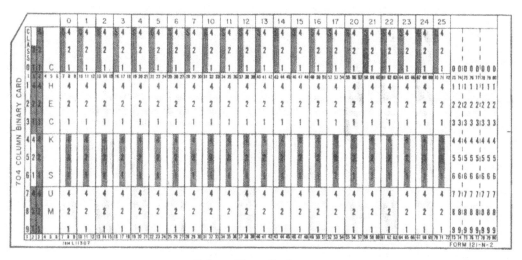

Column Binary Card

Row Binary Cards

There was another binary card format, row binary. Our online card reader read the first 72 columns of each card in row binary format. Each row held two words, starting with 9s-left, 9s-right, 8s-left, 8s-right, and so on up through the top row, 12s-right. The circled numbers are the decimal word numbers.

Column binary was much easier for us humans. Someone back in the days of the 704 had devised a 3-card loader. It bootstrapped itself into memory in row binary format, but it also contained instructions to rotate and unfold the matrices of the following cards, so that they could be punched as column binary.

Chapter 8: Programming in the 1960s and '70s

Soon after my transfer to Test Data Division in 1961, I was assigned to write two telemetry data unpacking programs. Missiles under test transmitted many thousands of measurements of various parameters (such as acceleration, vibration, pitch, yaw, temperature, and so on) as they streaked out across the Pacific Ocean. That telemetry data was transmitted to our headquarters in analog format. It was later digitized onto magnetic tape in gapless format (no inter-record gaps). The computer could read it from a 729 tape drive that had the gapless feature. At the risk of oversimplification, my two programs read the data from a special "gapless" tape drive, shifted and unscrambled the bits and converted them into floating-point values that our standard data processing programs could understand. I did not realize their importance at the time, but just did the best I could on these, my first two programs of consequence. As it turned out, they were used several times a day, at least for the seven years I worked there.

Pseudo-Coding

I was next asked to code a utility program to convert various number formats to BCD, so that they could be formatted for printing. The specifications were in the possession of a *program designer*. When I asked for them, he told me not to worry. He would give me *pseudo-code*, and I would convert each pseudo-instruction to an assembler statement. He had been an employee of the contractor, had converted to Civil Service, and asserted that was "how we always did it."

In other words, a program designer would create a flow chart and write, in English, a paraphrase to specify each computer operation. Then a *coder* would simply translate each pseudo-statement to an assembler statement.

I suggested to him and to management that he might as well have skipped the pseudo-code and written real code directly. That ended "the way we always did it." No more pseudo-code was written in our programming branch. Furthermore, instead of having a designer and a coder for each program to be written, we simply had one inventive programmer per program, who proudly designed, coded, documented, and debugged a finished product. Well, getting programmers to fully document their work was as difficult then as it is today.

Testing

New programmers are perfect optimists. It seems like everyone's very first program creates quite a shock when it crashes. It was supposed to be perfect! After we've written a few programs, we're not shocked or even surprised any more when they crash or malfunction.

My approach to testing was usually to start with the lowest-level modules and work upward. For each module, I would test first the main-line code and then, progressively, the more obscure paths. At the same time, I would usually test most variations of every parameter in the calling sequence.

The code to drive a particular test is sometimes discarded after the tested module behaves properly for that test case. Sometimes the code to drive the test has to be debugged first.

There is a finite limit to testing. Good judgment is required to decide an optimum limit. An unreasonably short time limit may cause important test cases to be skipped. Testing generally takes place after the program is already late. The potential consequences of a malfunction in production mode also affect the depth of testing.

When I was writing online programs (in the late '60s and early '70s) that processed terminal transactions, I tested very thoroughly. Then Dick, our systems programmer, would bring the program up in a testing mode and drop his open hand at random on the keyboard. A first-time programmer would protest that Dick wasn't supposed to do that. Dick would reply that it was just a matter of time before someone would do that, either on purpose, or accidentally. "Your program has to defend itself," he would say. "You can't let someone at a terminal crash your program by doing something you don't want to allow."

Operating Systems

SHARE Operating System (SOS)

In the early years through the 1950s, IBM was not in the software business and operating systems were custom and proprietary. Customers banded together to create SHARE, the organization of large-scale IBM computer users, as a forum in which to share technical information. Members of SHARE had cooperatively written the Share Operating System (SOS) for the 704, and later upgraded it for the 709.

Some companies did all the development and maintenance work, but many failed to do anything but use the fruits of others' labor. That led to pleas for IBM to take over system software development and include its cost in the price of the hardware, which finally happened in 1962.

Mock-Donald

For the 709 an improved control subsystem of SOS was named Mock-Donald after one of its creators, Clyde Mock. The Donald part of the name is yet another story:

> The 709 was capable of interleaving memory cycles between the central processor unit and the data channels for reading and writing external media, such as magnetic tape. A major function of the SOS upgrade was to overlap execution, input, and output. Execution (CPU) cycles were symbolized by E, input by I, and output by O. The development team further abbreviated the combination to EIO. Like most people, programmers have silly moments, and a team member came up with, "Old Mock Donald had a farm; E-I-E-I-O." From there, as the story goes, the name was born.

PMR was running a final field-test version of Mock Donald (MD) when I started in the Test Data Division in 1961.

Smasht

Some programmers at Johns Hopkins University later modified and improved Mock-Donald and named it *Smasht*, taken from their name for a new compression scheme for cards in a program "deck."

IBSYS

Around 1962, IBM replaced all those operating systems by releasing their first operating system, IBSYS. It contained the IBMAP (Macro Assembly Program) assembler, FORTRAN II, and a monitor subsystem for running programs. IBSYS was the beginning of *bundling*, the focus of anti-trust lawsuits against IBM a decade later.

SAP Assembler

Before IBSYS came along, we used SAP (the Share Assembly Program), originally written by United Aircraft as part of SOS for the 704. It created program code written in an assembler language called SCAT *(SHARE Compiler-Assembler-Translator)*.

SCAT used mnemonic operation codes *(opcodes)* for machine instructions, such as *CLA* for "Clear and Add" (Clear the accumulator register and add the contents of a specified storage location.) The equivalent instruction on S/360 (mid-1960s) was simply L for "Load." The 709 had over two hundred machine instructions. SCAT had a mnemonic opcode for each. A good applications programmer needed to know and use the mnemonics and instruction formats for about half of those. After a year or so, I became a systems programmer and, as such, knew and used nearly all of them. Our most valuable resource, in that regard, was the *IBM 709 Reference Manual*.

SAP also took care of address assignments and allowed us to use symbolic addresses (and address arithmetic that often got the programmer into trouble).

A Programmer's View of the IBM 709

The 709 had two computational 36-bit registers that a programmer could manipulate: the *accumulator* and the *MQ or multiplier/quotient*.

A third 36-bit register named the *Sense Indicators* could be loaded from memory or from 36 binary *sense switches* that could be set by the computer operator. A set of powerful Boolean instructions was available to test individual bits in that register to determine the operator's intent. The sense indicator register could also be used as 36 on-off program indicators, independent of the sense switches. In that case, programmers had the ability to test or set virtually any combination of bits.

The sense indicators were a powerful tool that I haven't seen on more recent computers; although I have no doubt that numerous command/control computers outside my experience have employed the equivalent.

The only other registers visible to the programmer were the *index registers*, a set of three 15-bit registers (0 to 32,767). They could be used to modify addresses and control loops, plus do a few other tasks if the programmer was clever. Sometimes we were too clever for our own good. Most of us finally learned to write straightforward code rather than clever code. When the 7094 came along, the number of index registers increased from three to seven, and we thought we were in heaven!

To Be a Systems Programmer

In 1962, when Wilson Cooper was promoted to become the technical manager of our Systems Programming Section, I took his prior position as the systems programmer for our proprietary operating system, working under him and with him.

Derisive Error Messages

Our operating system had been written by the contractor's two ace programmers. It had many messages written to define possible errors, such as in control cards. These punched cards were created by coders to run production jobs under control of the system. The systems programmer who created the messages had a somewhat theatrical bent. He suffixed all his control card error messages with a choice of several tart words. A message might read, "REQUESTED DEVICE MONU00 IS NON-EXISTENT. JOB TERMINATED. SHAME!" Another message would end with "PITY!" and so on.

Programmers should have a feeling of empathy in the creation of error messages. Lord knows we have caused enough of our own! The user is upset more than enough by his or her error, as explained in the message. "PITY!" really just rubs it in.

The star coder in the production section was named George. One evening, as he was hoping to get his last production job run and go home, he was faced with several error messages, each terminated with a sarcastic word. Faced with going home late and having a cold supper (before the age of microwave ovens), George shouted, "I'm going to smash that computer!" as he stomped off in the direction of the computer room (to which he would not have access, anyhow).

The result was manifold. George first had to be calmed. He next had to explain to his manager, who finally took George's side. Over the next day there came heated discussions between first- and second-level managers. The author of those messages, of course, had been gone to greener pastures for over a year. After a day or two of management discussion, the order came to me, the brand-new systems programmer, to "Rid the operating system of those vile epitaphs."

That was the easiest programming task I ever performed. I simply truncated the sarcasm from the end of each message (saving some valuable space, by the way). In the process, I learned the mechanics of modifying and testing the system.

Using the Sense Indicators—"Adjust"

My second systems programming assignment was as complex as the first was simple. Our many data processing programs expected the magnetic tapes they read as input to be in a format that was defined by a local standard.

I was to modify the system so that it would automatically detect and reformat several nonstandard tapes concurrently. I seem to recall that *Adjust* was the name of the program module that would do the reformatting. Wilson guided me in designing the interfaces to embed it into our data reduction operating system, with which I was just beginning to get acquainted. He then allowed me the liberty of the total design of the reformatting program.

I had long been fascinated by the potential of the sense indicators, and now I had the opportunity to really, really use them for something other than trivial tasks or communicating with the operator.

Speed was important, so I decided *Adjust* should be event-driven. I divided the sense indicators into four groups, with nine binary state indicators in each group. Each group drove a pair of tapes: one for input and one for the reformatted output.

I wanted them to compete for cycles asynchronously, but I also polled them in rotation to prevent any pair from being "locked out." One indicator would be set on completion of a *read* to indicate that a record was in an input buffer. The reformatting routine would soon get control. When it had prepared that record to write, it would set an indicator to be tested by the system's I/O control routines, which would start the output when the destination data channel and tape drive for that record were available. Nine Boolean indicators were just enough to control the process for one tape pair—input and output.

Thus, as many as four input tapes could be reformatted concurrently to their corresponding output tapes. They all competed for the three data channels and for memory cycles. When I had gotten through preliminary testing, I bravely loaded my new program down with a full complement of eight tape drives—16 spinning reels.

What a scene! The computer room seemed to explode, with eight type-729 tape drives apparently running simultaneously for minutes on end. On the 729, the spinning pair of 10½-inch feed and take-up reels was very visible, as were the two moving tape loops in glass-covered vacuum columns (which prevented the tape from being stretched or broken). Of course, they did not all move simultaneously, but they appeared to be doing so. The sight was complemented by the sound! As the orders to the tape drives were processed, the 16 feed and take-up relays made a greatly amplified staccato noise.

When I successfully ran out of test cases, I turned to George, with the consent of his manager. He created the most nightmarish test cases one could imagine, exposing another bug or two that my test cases had missed. Finally, *Adjust* was put into production, starting its illustrious career.

Adjust had another use we had never imagined! Every year, on Armed Forces Day, we had an open house. All classified media were secured and the computer room was opened up to the public.

Watching a computer was not very exciting. In prior years, we would set up some jobs to run programs that made the lights on the operator's console blink, and a couple tape drives spin. Imagine the new sensory phenomena with *Adjust* filling the computer room with a pretense of work on eight tape drives at once!

Fixing Channel Traps

My next project as systems programmer was one I chose: speed up the system by finding and fixing a bug related to channel trapping. It had caused the system to crash at random intervals, so channel traps had never been enabled in production jobs. To tell this story, I need to present a short tutorial about data channel traps and about Pacific Missile Range history.

At PMR the 709 computer had three IBM 7607 data channels connected to the processor. Peripheral devices were each wired to an assigned data channel. For example, several IBM 729 tape drives and other devices, such as the card reader or printer could be on channel A or B or C.

Each device had an assigned address that specified its channel and device address. When an I/O operation was initiated by an instruction in the central processing unit, the CPU would select the appropriate data channel, and then the channel would interpret the device address and select the appropriate device.

The data channels competed with each other and with the CPU for memory cycles. When a given channel selected a device to send or receive data, no other device on that channel could do so until the current operation was complete.

A data channel could *trap* the CPU on completion of an I/O operation—what programmers for most computers call an *interrupt*. An *interrupt* on the 709 meant that the CPU was canceling a data transfer operation (the CPU interrupting a channel and device), or that a control unit for a device on the channel was trying to get the attention of the channel.

When certain I/O operations, such as a read or write ended, and if channel trapping was enabled, the following would happen:

- Channel trapping would automatically become inhibited (to prevent trapping the trap-processing routine).
- Control would be taken from the program currently executing.
- The program's linkage and status would be automatically stored.
- Control would pass to a particular location in low storage, depending upon the channel. Each of those locations would contain an unconditional transfer to the appropriate trap processor routine for that channel.

Now comes the bit of history. Before PMR had the large scale 709 computer, an IBM 650 medium-sized computer was used for the same purpose for several years. The 709 was a recent acquisition, and the proprietary operating system was fairly new (created by the two ace programmers I referred to a few pages back). They had most of their bugs fixed by the time we took over, but one in particular required a workaround.

The bug reared its ugly head at random times, and the workaround (that they had implemented) had been to disable channel traps. In other words, there was a bug in the trap processing routine.

When channel traps were working properly, the system was maybe twice as efficient (a guess on my part) as when traps were inhibited, so trapping was very desirable. That rationale was how I sold my manager on letting me spend valuable time to find and fix the bug that had defied our predecessors. Remember that, even with channel traps inhibited, the 709 processed data much faster than the older, smaller, slower 650.

When channel trapping was enabled and a read operation (for example) completed, the trap routine would dispatch the I/O control program in the system's nucleus to set a flag, so that the current program would know that the I/O was complete.

In that way, the program could process that new record. Before returning control, the trap routine would also give the I/O control routine an immediate chance to start any waiting I/O operation before returning to the program.

Without channel trapping, the system eventually learned of the new status by polling—that is, by looping through instructions to test the channels for each active I/O device until it discovered that an operation was complete. That was a slow way of operating.

I found the bug by inspecting the author's code and "playing computer" in my head. Simply stated, channel trapping was enabled five instructions too soon, which allowed the trap routine to be trapped before restoring the status and linkage back to the original program, a disastrous no-no.

I must add that there was significant uncertainty, on my part, as to whether I had really found the problem. "This was too easy," I thought in my heart. My head contradicted my heart, saying that I had found and fixed the problem. Only after the fix had successfully passed the dynamic tests that I put it through for several days did I allow myself a big "whew." Most bugs are miniscule but their effects are profound!

Computer Operations

Our locally-written system ran at least twenty hours a day to support our missile data reduction jobs. Dozens of measuring instruments on a missile, sometimes sending thousands of readings a second as it streaked out across the Pacific Ocean, sent voluminous telemetry data back to us.

It was the job of a couple hundred specialized programs, running under our proprietary operating system, to translate and summarize those readings into a form that humans could comprehend. Added to the telemetry data was trajectory data from numerous cinetheodolites (special movie cameras showing azimuth and elevation) and radar sites that tracked each missile.

Production Jobs

Our group of coders worked in shifts around the clock, seven days a week. They wrote *Job Control Language*, or JCL, a term that was later coined to do very similar functions in OS/360 (the operating system for the S/360 computer) starting in the mid-'60s. A typical JCL punched card would specify a program to read data from a specified magnetic tape, do its unique manipulation of the data, and write the result back to another specified tape. Then another program would be called to do its thing, and another, and so on until all the final data was formatted on tape. Some of it was on archive tapes and some was in report form to be sent to the printer.

Our operating system's job was to interpret the JCL, to check for coding errors, to invoke the specified programs in the proper sequence with the correct data, and to provide utility functions such as data conversion routines and input/output buffering routines as needed by each data reduction program.

Magnetic Tape Problems

Most operating systems had moderate provisions in their code for recovery from errors on magnetic tape. Ours was more sophisticated because of the volume of tape data processed, and it would become even more so after we upgraded our tape drives to 800 bits per inch (bpi), stating how many 6-bit rows of data there could be on an inch of tape.

We were heavy users of tape data. We had a very large tape library where data was archived and *scratch tapes* were also stored. A scratch tape could be a brand-new blank tape, but more often it was an old archive tape that had been released for reuse.

When we upgraded our tape drives from 200 bpi to 556 bpi, we were able to use most of the 200 bpi reels of tape at 556 bpi, even though they were not certified for that. So, imagine the rationale of the Computer Operations manager when we were to acquire new tape drives at 800 bpi: "It worked once, so it will work again." When the new drives were installed, we immediately had serious problems, but there wasn't money in his budget to buy all new 800 bpi tapes.

The operations manager pointed his finger at the IBM model 729 tape drives. IBM pointed at PMR's tapes, not certified at 800 bpi. With an impasse between IBM and the Operations Branch, our Programming Branch manager told Wilson to have us find the problem and fix it. The job was delegated to me.

I started by writing a diagnostic program that would give me a chance to count the errors on a bad tape that the operators set aside for me. In any 24-hour period, the operators would generally provide me with at least a couple bad tapes. About mid-morning they would stop production and give me the computer for a half hour or so. Through the sense switches on the operator's console, I could tell the program to stop the tape at any error. I would isolate a few inches of tape around a selected error and then take a scissors to that tiny section of the 2400-foot tape. That usually spelled the death of that reel of tape, a sacrifice of a few tapes to save many. After giving the computer back to the operators, I would take the bad tape sections into a work room. Our Customer Engineer and I would sprinkle a bad spot with MagniSee, a fine iron powder. We tapped it lightly so that the powder would align to the magnetic bits. Then we transferred the powder to the sticky side of some transparent tape. With the help of the cinetheodolite film processing department, we magnified the bad section—anywhere from a fraction of an inch to a few inches—times 200. We could actually see the bad bit patterns.

When a writing error was encountered, a standard error recovery, or "*badspot*" routine, would get control and backspace over the bad record, write a 3½-inch blank space starting where the bad record had been, and rewrite the record past that.

We discovered a big problem. When a tape drive was rewriting a tape and detected an error, control would be transferred to the badspot routine, which—we finally discovered—would replace the erroneous bits with its own error, undetected at that time. In a later task, when the record was read, the second error would set off another error recovery effort—a read error that had been caused by a triangular wedge of data that had been written previously under control of the write recovery routine.

We determined that the problem was caused when the tape was written. When a tape blemish was detected in writing a record, the tape backspaced over that record. When it did a high-speed reversal of tape motion to write blank tape, the drive rollers skewed (slightly twisted) the tape and failed to erase a tiny triangle of data. This seemed to be a problem on the tape drives in general. The engineers at IBM's tape drive laboratory were amazed.

We didn't have time to wait for a fix from IBM. I modified the badspot-write routine to back up one more record (over a good one), then forward space over that good record before writing the blank tape. That made the bulk of our tape problems recoverable until, finally, most of the old tapes had been replaced by new ones certified at 800 bpi.

Computer Room Procedures

Up through the 1960s and '70s, the typical programmer was not allowed in the computer room, but rather depended upon computer room clerks and computer operators to execute their programs.

Submitting a Job

The mechanics of writing and testing a program required the programmer to:

1. **Get a pad of 8½"x11" coding sheets** designed for the programming language to be used. Eighty columns would be broken into fields pertinent to that language.

2. **Write the program on the sheets.** We learned to leave many blank lines for unanticipated statements to be filled in as the program developed. Rare was the programmer who never had to rewrite most of a sheet of statements to squeeze one or two more lines in. Most of us used mechanical pencils so we could change our minds and correct errors. I knew only one programmer who coded in ink.

3. **Fill out a job request form and submit the sheets** of statements to be punched into 80-column IBM cards by keypunch operators, generally women who worked in shifts around the clock. Keypunching was their full-time job, day after day, month after month. If we submitted our keypunch job before going home for the night, it was usually ready the next morning.

4. **Pick up the box or boxes of cards** (up to 2000 cards per box) at the computer room output window when they were done. A typical program would take perhaps a thousand cards, which would be approximately a 9" deck, too many cards to hold with one hand without big rubber bands around them.

5. **Put control cards on the front to invoke the assembler or compiler** to be used, and on the back to invoke test cases we had chosen.

6. **Submit the job to a computer room clerk** to have full-time computer operators run it. Any extraordinary actions directed at the operator had to be spelled out in meticulous detail.

7. **Pick up the results of the test job.** This would include the input deck, printed output, and perhaps a compressed output deck (compressed decks will be explained in a page or so). We might wait for an hour or a day or more.

8. **Correct the errors (*bugs*) found**, maybe waiting in line to use the only self-service keypunch, in order to punch a few cards.

9. **Resubmit the job for retest.** The most we could hope for was to run two or three tests per day; sometimes it was two days per test.

A good programmer would have "fill work" to do while waiting for computer jobs. That might be documenting the program, keeping up with trade publications, or working on other programs.

Those of us who had learned to write code in small single-function modules usually had some code to write while testing one or two other modules. You could tell who the most efficient programmers were: they were always busy.

I remember a conversion task in the 1970s where we had to modify dozens of programs to run under a different operating system. I had a chart that showed the conversion and test status of ten to twenty programs that I was working on, three or four at any point in time when it was taking a day or two to run a test.

Compressed Card Decks

Our SCAT language processors could reduce the number of cards needed to reassemble a program. They could encode a string of two or more identical characters, such as blanks, into a two-character field. This and other techniques in their algorithms allowed them to output a deck of card images (yes, on tape, to be punched off-line) that was typically 40% of the size of the original deck.

Sequence numbers were punched automatically into the cards of compressed decks, so if one did accidentally shuffle the deck, it was more easily sorted into its original sequence.

The advantages were primarily space and program integrity.

- **Space and weight:** If some of a programmer's Hollerith card decks—those that were encoded on keypunches by the keypunch ladies—filled five card drawers (say, 15,000 cards), then their replacement compressed decks would take only about two drawers. I don't have any idea of the weight taken off the floor, but it sure reduced problems on floors not made of concrete. For our group of three, it would free up six feet of valuable wall space.
- **Program Integrity:** Although our original Hollerith cards (the keypunched ones) had a *card sequence field* in columns 73 to 80, it was seldom used because of the cost for the keypunch lady to manually punch those columns.

Occasionally, someone would drop a deck of cards. It was easy. If not wrapped in rubber bands, nobody would try to pick up a whole deck of 1000 cards—it was just too big—but they might try 500. (I had big hands and could hold about 500 cards in one hand.) However, if they were not sequenced, dropping them was a catastrophe that would cost hours or days to rearrange, so we would pick up smaller bunches.

MockDonald could create a SQUOZE deck for you encoded in biquinary, a hybrid of the base-5 number system practically unreadable by mere humans.

When we wanted to modify a SQUOZE deck, we would keypunch ALTER cards and put them on the front of the deck. They contained the statement numbers where we wanted to add, delete, or replace, followed by our new Hollerith cards for additions or replacements. INTRAN, which read the decks, knew how to make sense out of all that. It would modify the card images accordingly and pass them on to the assembler. OUTRAN could then create a replacement SQUOZE deck if we so indicated.

When the programmers at Johns Hopkins University modified Mock-Donald, they created—among other changes—an improved compressed deck encoding scheme and called it SMASHT.

When IBM created IBSYS, it used yet another scheme for compressing decks of cards and called it PREST.

Laughable Situations

Programmers enjoy laughs as much as any folks and work provided many laughable occasions.

"I Am Here"

We had provisions for *tracing* in our testing via a routine in SOS (SHARE Operating System) called SNAP. Programmers could insert statements in their code to produce identifying information to be printed off-line by a function named SNAP-TRAN. If there were several such paths to be traced, then the programmer would tailor each tracing statement to identify that particular location, along with other desired information, such as the contents of registers or specified storage locations.

One morning a programmer (not me, by the grace of God) picked up his overnight output at the Operations window. It included thousands of pages of the same short message: "I am here," where each "here" *should* have specified its particular location. All his different "*here's*" looked the same and his test was wasted, along with all the paper. The story spread like wildfire, and his naiveté was obvious to the entire cadre of programmers. One hopefully never repeats such an error.

The Tipsy Cabinet

We learned, early on, not to open more than one or two drawers in a card cabinet at once. One of my co-workers had played football for Purdue. I heard him shout for help in the next office one day. I rushed to see what had happened. He was trying to apply a body block on a dozen or more card drawers that had all started to open when the cabinet had tipped forward. Thankfully, the tipping had stopped when the bottom drawers jammed on the floor. The two of us wrestled it back to level. As soon as we accomplished that, it became funny, and I've laughed about it ever since.

Personal Experiences

In 1962, when I became the systems programmer for our locally-written operating system, it began to sink into my head that systems programmers were often called to isolate or find someone else's problem when all else failed. Sometimes it was simply to discover whose program caused the problem. I also discovered that application programmers liked to point the blame at the system or at the computer. Systems programmers often had to find the real culprits to protect their own reputations.

Along with the responsibilities and consequences came some special privileges. For example, I had direct access to the computer room and the computer, whenever it was justified.

Normally we used standard tracing tools and techniques to isolate bugs, but more than once I gave the computer operators a chance for a long break while I took over the computer and stepped it through one instruction at a time in single-cycle mode to find a problem. A few of those turned out to be strange hardware problems.

Because every minute—indeed, every second—of time on the computer was so expensive, my early tendency was to rush whenever I had the computer in single-cycle mode. I soon learned to take the time I needed to think as I proceeded. It was too easy to inadvertently bounce past the bug after spending five precious minutes getting to it.

My Only Bug-Free Program?

Perhaps the hardest early lesson for new programmers (even today) is that, no matter how confident they are in their code, they must expect some bugs.

Indeed, even for thoroughly-tested and "proven" programs, some veteran programmers will state that there are still likely bugs in the code, and it's a matter of time before they show up.

I was discussing that theory with another programmer one day in the early 1960s. I had a simple little utility subroutine of perhaps forty instructions to write. He was willing to bet me *big money* that I could not write it without a bug. I spent a full eight hours on that routine, much of it "playing computer" to find bugs before I sent it in. I had taken it as a dare, but my confidence was indicated by the size of the bet I was willing to make—a cup of coffee. Well, I won! It could be the only bug-free code I ever wrote. Or was it really bug-free? Would time tell on me?

The Dropped Bit

One morning an engineer picked up his computer output, including some printed reports, from the operations folks. He discovered some impossible values. We later determined that those numbers were in a certain range, and each was printed as half the value of what it really was. The author of the report program was given the problem to find and fix, but by mid-morning he threw up his hands in despair. His lack of findings only served to put the integrity of both the hardware and the operating system into question, so Wilson and I were called in to find the problem posthaste, no matter who or what caused it!

From the symptoms, we initially thought it was a *software* problem. The two of us worked with the application programmer to narrow it down. After an hour or so, we isolated it to a few instructions and single-cycled the computer through them, finally learning that it was a *hardware* problem. There was a malfunction associated with one bit of core memory out of more than a million bits (32,768 36-bit words). Some instructions (perhaps all but one) sensed the presence of a 1-bit there, but one particular instruction did not. At that point we summoned the IBM hardware guy (in those days called a *Customer Engineer*). The exact problem was unbelievable to him until we proved it. At that point, still scratching his head, he set about to fix it.

Bitten By a Relative Address

Too often, programmers got into trouble using address arithmetic. One address problem brought my boss's boss, an applications programmer, and me out to work for several hours in the middle of the night. The adventure started around seven p.m. when the computer halted for an unknown reason. Yes, the 709x could halt.

The computer operator determined that it was trying to execute an opcode of all zeros down in the operating system's area of memory. 0000_8 was the instruction HTR (HALT AND TRANSFER). The privilege of halting the computer was reserved for a few events in the operating system, and this was not one of them.

Operations called the branch manager who called me at my home. (Wilson got to stay home.) I found that a certain application program had taken a wild transfer (on most computers it is called a branch). We called that program's maintenance programmer at his home and he came in. By that time it was nearing midnight, and data reduction for a missile launch scheduled for the wee hours was being threatened by the problem.

One thing I learned early on in finding problems was to ask, "What did you change?" and that was my first question of him.

"I didn't change anything," he replied.

"Let me look at your listing."

He went to his office and brought back the listing of the program's code.

"I thought you said you hadn't changed it," I said, pointing to that day's date on the assembler listing of his program.

"Oh, I just added an instruction."

"Did you test it?"

"No. It was an innocuous change that would never cause a problem. I just inserted a *Set Sign Plus* instruction in a calculation that needed an absolute value."

Now mind you, our SCAT assembler would allow us to assign a label to any statement in any program we wrote. Yet, it was not uncommon for a programmer to use *address arithmetic* to refer to an unlabeled statement—either an instruction or data. Perhaps it was laziness, or maybe it was being macho, but it invited disaster if an instruction was inserted or deleted in that range.

We discovered that he had unknowingly put the SSP instruction smack dab in the middle of the relative address range of a transfer instruction. Its presence accidentally caused the transfer to be made to the wrong instruction, which caused a couple more wild transfers, ending up trying to execute a data location down in the operating system. After a quick repair and test, the preparations for the launch's data reduction were resumed.

The programmer, in this case, was somewhat of a victim. Someone else had written the program, and this guy inherited it because the author had left our employ. The new guy was naïve enough to fall into a trap when he had to make this particular modification. Then he made the error critical by not testing the change, however innocent-looking.

73

I wish I could say we learned not to do that kind of thing. I have seen other generations of programmers—obviously not adequately trained—repeat the same poor programming practices.

Trap Transfer Mode

One time I was trying to track down an error in someone's program. They had given up. It was causing a wild transfer to location 0, a data word which, if accidentally executed, contained zeros in the opcode field, a real show-stopper. Luckily, someone had figured out a workaround (a way to avoid the error temporarily), so we had some time. That was a good thing. The problem took a couple weeks to solve, in between my other duties.

I finally found his problem in a seldom-used branch of code in a processing loop. The program only failed with a certain set of data. We had tried taking debug snapshots, but that became impractical because of volume. It processed tens of thousands of data points in a loop before abruptly crashing.

I thought about a 709x feature called *Trap Transfer Mode*. I never heard of anyone else, including systems programmers, who ever used it. I decided it was the best hope for finding the guy's bug. It was simple in concept. There was an instruction to set Trap Transfer Mode On, which would cause any transfer—except one—to *trap* to a fixed location in low memory. Another location contained the linkage to the transfer causing the trap.

I wrote an interpreter for all the possible transfer instructions. It could link to a routine that would do whatever tests I wanted it to do, and take an action I specified when and if the tests were satisfied. Each time the tests were not satisfied, it would return control to my interpreter, which would then set all the registers and indicators to what they would have been otherwise, turn trapping back on, and then execute a *Trap Transfer* to the original transfer instruction's intended location. TTR was the one transfer that was immune to trapping.

After I got my trapping code working, I converged on the guy's problem rather quickly. *Quickly* is a relative term here. My trap routine slowed the computer to a small fraction of its normal speed through the program, but it finally led me to identify the problem. A certain range of values in the incoming data caused execution of a branch of code, never before invoked, that contained the bug. That's all! Finding a problem is usually the major part of the effort. Fixing it is often trivial. The programmer then had to test the fix, another matter that often takes a substantial effort.

I had fixed several of my own bugs in my interpreter's code, but I finally was stymied. After tracing through thousands of transfers, the computer left transfer trapping mode when it shouldn't have, and my interpreter ceased to gain control. In order to find the bug in the guy's program, I had to find and fix my own problem. I finally narrowed it down to one instruction, RQL 34, an innocent instruction in the program that rotated the MQ register 34 bits. When the computer executed that instruction, it also turned transfer trapping off, which it was not supposed to do.

I created a tiny little test case, so I could demonstrate the problem to our IBM Customer Engineer. I had his confidence, having helped him isolate numerous hardware problems and written a number of diagnostic programs for him. He was, nevertheless, astounded. He then found it to be a wiring error and fixed the problem that very day. I wonder if he is still shaking his head about it. I always wondered how many of our computer's sisters had the same wiring error.

Outsmarted by My Own Program

I've been outsmarted by my own program more than once in my career. It would generally be when I was testing a new program. Thinking I had given it a request to do one thing, I found it did what I told it to do, not what I *thought* I had told it to do.

One occasion I remember well was when three of us—Wilson, a co-worker, and I—were writing a new, more efficient operating system (circa 1964) to replace our old one. One particular function was a so-called *Device Allocator*, which I had created. Its job was to convert requests for "symbolic" input/output devices in computerized data reduction jobs into physical assignments. Most of these were our dozen-plus magnetic tape drives.

Short of using several pages to explain it, I'll simply state that many such assignments could not be solved by the algorithm used on the old system. Those computer jobs had to be broken into multiple simpler jobs at great expense. My task was to create a much improved—iterative—scheme, which I did. Testing started with very simple test cases and developed, as I found and fixed bugs, into more comprehensive trials. I had finally gotten to the point where I was satisfied with its performance.

I then created a few more test cases that were "impossible" to solve. I wanted to test and debug the error-handling routines that would be invoked. At least one of those resulted in a successful set of assignments.

"Uh, oh," I thought, "Why did it fail to recognize that it couldn't do this?"

As I analyzed the assignments it had made, I came to the realization that the impossible was possible after all, and my code had discovered a solution that I, myself, could not.

I imagine that, if you asked a dozen software engineers about this type of experience, several would have their own stories to tell.

The Advent of Compilers

In 1961 a few of our programmers started to use FORTRAN. Others of us looked down our noses at such "inefficient usage of memory and computer cycles." Memory was still very expensive. It took years for memories to grow, cycles to shorten, and some of us to be converted.

The COmmon Business-Oriented Language (COBOL) had also been under development in the 1950s. It was to become an industry-wide commercial application counterpart to FORTRAN, which served the scientific community.

Sometime in 1961, unaware of the COBOL compiler, I recommended use of a compiler named ComTran (IBM's commercial application compiler) for use on a new application. Shortly thereafter we got a COBOL compiler, and I am supposing ComTran soon became the world's first obsolete compiler. I had to "eat" my earlier recommendation, and one of our programmers had to rewrite the application in COBOL in order to add new features.

Though compiled programs took more precious space and ran considerably slower than assembler programs, they were much faster to debug because they were closer to human language and, therefore, had fewer errors.

Absolute Programs

The 709x series of computers had no such thing as a *base register*.

Until IBSYS came along, our programs were said to be *absolute*. When we assembled or compiled a program, we established the exact memory locations where it would be loaded and executed. These were generally standard locations dictated by the operating system. For example, the operating system for our missile data reduction jobs restricted itself to the first 7000 words in the 709x. All of our application programs were loaded into location 7000_{10} and up.

I was that system's maintenance programmer for three years. There were about 15,000 instructions, arranged in overlays; that is, different parts were loaded at different times. I had to be clever enough, when adding code for new features, to keep the ends of the overlays below location 7000_{10} because there were about 200 application programs (written and maintained by a few dozen programmers) that all started at 7000_{10}, and moving them all would have been totally unacceptable.

Bear in mind that the 709x computers were not created for multitasking, so when a certain program was given control, it used the whole computer exclusively until it was finished. The system provided utilities for buffered reading and writing, for number system conversions, and for other functions that an application could call as subroutines with standard linkages.

Our homebrew system did not assemble or compile programs. All our assemblies were done in the early days by the Share Operating System and during my first couple years by the Mock-Donald version of SOS. FORTRAN had started out all alone, as a lonesome compiler in its own Fortran Monitor System (FMS) in 1956–57, written originally for the IBM 704 computer.

In 1962 we installed the fruits of IBM's labor: the results of its effort to replace SOS, Mock-Donald, and SMASHT with its own bundled product named IBSYS. It had several subsystems that ran under its umbrella. One was the IBMAP (Macro Assembly Program) assembler which was upward compatible with, and replaced, all previous SCAT language assemblers. Another contained the FORTRAN compiler.

Relocatable Programs

One of the new goals of IBSYS was to support program relocation. That was challenging, to say the least, with no more than a few index registers to effect dynamic address modification (and not for all instructions). In any case, index registers were too precious to give even one away to the operating system, so how did they do it?

Binary card decks were the media used to contain newly-assembled or compiled programs. We would copy a deck onto a library tape for production work. IBM devised a scheme to encode *relocatable* addresses in the deck so that the program loader would recognize them. The loader, knowing the base location for that particular load, would add that to each address flagged as relocatable.

IBM's first effort to produce a relocatable loader resulted in a snail, so to speak. It seemed to take forever to load a program. As it was read, each address field had to be tested for relocatability and modified if so indicated.

At a SHARE meeting in Philadelphia, I had a conversation with one of a team of three programmers of a large IBM customer who rewrote that loader to keep up with the normal I/O speed, that is, the speed of reading the program from tape. I never learned whether IBM bought the code or reinvented it.

The real point of this little story is that three very talented programmers without the burden of a bureaucracy could do a better job faster than two departments of programmers that had to follow lots of rules. This is not to embarrass IBM, where I later spent a quarter century working, but rather to document the efficiency of a small, proficient, tight-knit, and creative group.

Database—Ahead of Its Time

Around 1964, four of us at the Pacific Missile Range headquarters sat down to specify a set of data files that would let us program important new reports. What we were trying to create would, a few years later, be called a Relational Database, but we didn't get so far as to give it a name. All we had was a 1301 disk and some tape drives. The disk capacity was far too limited for the amount of data required. The project was postponed indefinitely. Three years later when I changed employers, it was still not feasible so I do not know what ever happened to our idea.

Improved Programming Techniques

I have touched on several poor programming practices, but perhaps the worst, in my view, was so-called spaghetti code. Throughout my career, one of the most error-prone practices that I observed was non-modular code—up to thousands of instructions in some cases. Sometimes this code was written off the top of the author's head, skipping much of the design step. Branches were sometimes made from a conditional or unconditional branch to an instruction ten (yes, even a hundred) pages away in the listing.

The author of spaghetti code had a substantially harder challenge when it was time to debug the code. It was even worse six months or a year later when some new function was to be added to the code. By that time, the author had forgotten much of the more dangerous nuances of that program's code. Not only would they create more bugs than necessary, but they would now add more spaghetti. The original authors of many programs were no longer there after a year or two. Pity the new programmer trainee whose first task it was to modify such a program.

In the early 1970s a number of improved programming technologies saw widespread exposure in the industry. The Association for Computing Machinery (ACM) had been promoting such techniques as Modular Design and Structured Programming since the mid-sixties, perhaps earlier. Their combined voice and others finally made an impression on managers, who finally sent their programmers to class to improve their techniques.

Modular Programs

I learned the term Modular Programming in the early 1970s. When I looked to see what it was about, my comment was, "I've been doing this for ten years." Three of us had written an operating system of many thousands of instructions back in the early-to-mid sixties. It was made of many modules—each with a precise function—of which few required more than a couple of pages to list the (assembler, not compiler) instructions. They each had one entry point and a single exit through a standard linkage to the calling routine. Perhaps we were ahead of the curve.

Structured Programming

The other "improved" technique was *Structured Programming*. Its effect was to contain each kernel of logic by means of a few structures. It was new to us largely because, as assembler programmers, we were not accustomed to "IF...THEN...ELSE" constructs and "DO" loops. We were given macros to create the equivalent structures in assembler language, and before long we had mastered it.

In 1976 I transferred to a project to create a subsystem requiring tight code. I learned to use a proprietary in-house compiler designed expressly for systems programming. This made structured programming easier than in assembler code. When necessary I could invoke its feature to generate a small segment of my own assembler code. Little did I know at the time that I was destined to write tens of thousands of code statements in that language for several different computers over the next fifteen years.

Association for Computing Machinery

During my first decade in the business, roughly between 1960 and 1970, the number of computers in the world increased from 10,000 to 100,000.

By the mid-1960s, computers were showing up at manufacturers and "think tanks" on the Central Coast. I was fortunate to help a few programming professionals from those installations to co-found the Santa Barbara Chapter of the Association for Computing Machinery and recruit several charter members from my programming group at PMR.

Chapter 9: The Evolution of Peripherals

Data on Disks

In the 1950s, IBM had leased space for a laboratory with a special purpose in downtown San Jose, California. Its initial mission was to determine the feasibility of storing data in concentric tracks on a magnetic surface of a flat disk. In doing this, it became the birthplace of RAMAC (Random Access Method of Accounting), its successors, and therefore, of the computer age's magnetic disk industry.

A manufacturing plant was built on a large parcel of land at (what was then) the south end of San Jose. That plant, whose primary purpose was to design and build magnetic disk storage media, spawned the new disk storage industry.

Serial versus Random Access

Up until that time our data (other than data punched into cards) had been stored on magnetic tapes.

Data was stored serially on those tapes. Records of arbitrary lengths were stored, one after another, in files, also of arbitrary lengths. Between each record was a short blank area (about ¾ inch) in which the tape could either accelerate or decelerate between a stop and read/write speed. Between each file was a larger blank area (3½ inches) preceded by a specially-encoded magnetic marker. This arrangement worked well for data that was to be accessed serially, that is, records 1, 2, 3, 4, and so on.

Our old operating systems were based on tape. To get from record 1 to 100, records 2 through 99 had to be spaced over—a big waste of time if one did not need the data in those records at that moment. For example, one may need to load an error-recovery module that is hundreds of records distant on tape. Even with schemes that took advantage of high-speed spacing over files, it was a time-consuming activity.

Disks, on the other hand, are random access devices. Several records are written on each of many concentric tracks. Picture yourself with a CD or DVD, jumping to the track on which a new tune or scene starts. This is called random access because you can instantly skip all the data on the tracks in between. A computer disk works in similar fashion.

The IBM 350 (RAMAC) and 355

September 4, 1956 was the announcement day of IBM's RAMAC (*Random Access Method of Accounting*) and, therefore, of the magnetic disk industry. The IBM 305 (RAMAC) was a data processing system whose revolutionary feature was the IBM 350 disk storage unit. The 350 was so vital to RAMAC that the industry soon referred to the 350, itself, as the RAMAC. The 350 did away with the need to continually process and store punched cards, and greatly increased speed.

In 1960, while I was still working for the Management Data Processing Department (with Electric Accounting Machinery) at the Pacific Missile Range, our IBM salesman arranged for a tour of the Ventura County Accounting Department for my manager, my manager's manager, and me. The purpose was to show us their RAMAC. The 350 disk storage unit was about 5 feet long, a bit taller than that, and about 2 or 3 feet deep and, we were told, weighed more than a ton. It had 50 disks, each somewhat less than a foot in diameter. It could hold 5 million characters (approximately 5 MB) which, today, would fit into a person's pocket.

The 350 used air pressure to move the actuator, which would position the single read/write head in two steps. First, it would position adjacent to the specified disk surface, then over the specified track. Seek time (time to move to another track) averaged between a half second and a second.

We were impressed by the RAMAC's performance (compared to randomly accessed data on serial tape drives). It was shortly before I transferred to the Range Operations Department, so I do not know what MDPD finally did about it.

The IBM 355 was announced ten days after the announcement for RAMAC. The 355 connected to the IBM 650, storing six million decimal digits.

Little did I know that, three years later, I would be one of the first to program their successor, the IBM 1301.

The IBM 353, 1301 and 1302

The 353, with the same basic design as the 1301, was made for use with the IBM 7030 computer. Its capacity was about two million words of 64 bits plus 8 parity bits. The 1301 was announced in June 1961, the 1302 about two years later. The 1302's capacity was quadruple that of the 1301.

In late 1963, a short time after we got our first 7094 computer, I was told that we were to be the third customer to lease IBM's 1301 disk drive. With all due respect to its predecessor, the RAMAC, I believe the 1301 was the product that fueled the early stage of the explosive growth of the disk business.

A cabinet about three feet square and perhaps six feet tall could contain two 1301 disk units, one above the other. The control unit was in an attached cabinet of about the same size. A 1301 consisted of a stack of twenty-one disks (using forty surfaces). Each was about a quarter inch thick and over two feet in diameter. Each surface could contain as much as 18,600 36-bit words. The 1301's theoretical capacity was 744,000 words, or 4,464,000 6-bit characters at about $26,000 per million characters. Today you could put that data (and more!) in your pocket on one inexpensive flash drive. At the time, the disk drive's capacity was barely believable for me.

The idea of putting our operating system, program library, and certain other files onto disk had great promise, and we would not be disappointed! Wilson Cooper and I went to IBM's very first 1301 programming class. Only a handful of people— mostly in IBM's development laboratories—had actually written code for the 1301, and they were mostly product developers, not teachers.

Over the next month, the two of us wrote assembler code to format the 1301, to put our proprietary operating system and program library onto it, to load the system and any selected application program into the 7094's memory from disk, and to perform disk error recovery functions. We coded the main processor's I/O instructions, commands for the 7909 Data Channel, and orders for the 1301's control unit. The only 1301 existing outside of IBM's labs was a beta-test model at Western Data Processing Center (UCLA) in Los Angeles. We rented one-hour blocks of computer time there to test our code, removing bugs until it worked.

File Allocation

One of us (probably Wilson, because I do not remember doing it) invented an algorithm for keeping track of used space versus unused space on the disk. When a certain amount of space was needed to write a record, our subroutine would allocate it from a table of unused space. The authors of OS/360 invented generalized schemes to do the same. Finally, Marc McDonald designed a *File Allocation Table* standard for personal computers that is still in use today.

Debugging for the IBM 1301

Our first code to test was that which formatted the disks. Wilson Cooper reminds me, these many years later, that, "I recall that our first run of the 1301 format program at UCLA/WDPC went fine until it found an unrecoverable error on one of the last cylinders (#199?). The next day [our IBM liaison] reported that, sure enough, the 1301 had a problem on that cylinder. Was that another bug-free program?"

The mechanics of debugging were another matter. We rented two one-hour blocks of time per day, leaving several days in between each of those to keep up with our other duties at Point Mugu. We'd leave Point Mugu shortly after eight o'clock for the trip to UCLA, and our first hour started at ten. We had a box of 10½-inch reels of tape. When the system was released to us we mounted the tapes on at least six IBM 729 tape drives. We did this rather crisply, by a procedure we had agreed upon, since every minute was important and expensive. We would IPL (boot, literally Initial Program Load) the system and run the first test we had prepared and then the second, time permitting, and so on until our hour was up. Then we would take the tapes containing snapshots of selected memory, registers, and "core dumps" (dumps of all 32K words of the memory's magnetic cores at the time of a program crash) to be printed off-line. That was a good time to relax and eat our bag lunches.

After a short lunch, we would spread our data out on a big table in a nearby workroom that was at our disposal, find bugs, and make keypunch fixes for as many as possible. When our second hour came at two o'clock, we repeated the morning's general procedure until our hour was up. Then we'd pack up and return to Point Mugu to unload. After about three trips to UCLA, our system passed all our tests.

Our 1301 and its associated boxes arrived on schedule. The Customer Engineering team installed it on a weekend, working Sunday night and through the wee hours. IBM's 1301 diagnostic programs were so new that they were not completely debugged yet. They flagged some "errors" in places that the meters and oscilloscopes said were okay.

Wilson and I arrived about five or six o'clock Monday morning. About seven o'clock, in desperation, the Customer Engineers had us try our recently-tested code.

It and the disk drive worked just fine! After resolving some minor control card problems, we successfully formatted the 1301 and loaded the operating system onto it. About eight o'clock, as the day shift computer operators came on duty, we put our new disk-based operating system into production-test mode. I think we ran the old tape-based system only once after that, about a year later when the 1301 was down for the replacement of a major part, the actuator.

Talk about an increase in speed! It had sometimes taken over a minute to search past ¼ mile of tape on the library reel to find and load a specified program. The disk drive reduced that time to about a second. The 1301 repaid its monthly lease cost almost immediately through increased production. The time to run one particular job, an extreme case that searched a library tape extensively, went from more than three minutes to less than ten seconds. I thought it had terminated prematurely until I inspected the output data.

Hydraulic Actuators

Data on a disk is arranged in concentric circles, or *tracks*. The read and write heads are on a slide assembly (*actuator*) that can position the heads over any track.

In the 1301 the actuator moved by means of hydraulic fluid pressure. In order to position the heads accurately, the fluid temperature had to be constant throughout the lines in which it was contained. As long as it was in use, the fluid circulated enough to keep the temperature uniform and there were no problems, but after an extended period of non-use, it would fail to position the heads accurately. The immediate fix was to order it to *re-zero*, an operation that caused the fluid to recirculate, with all valves open, for about five seconds. I created a tiny (three-card) binary combination bootstrap/program deck so the computer operators could re-zero the 1301 when they needed to. For such limited use, the snail-paced online card reader was valuable.

Fusing a Wire Together

About a year after the 1301 installation (and after IBM's IBSYS conversion to run off of it), operations complained one day that IBSYS was reporting an unidentified unrecoverable error, so nobody could assemble or compile a program. Roger, our Customer Engineer, called to ask me to help identify the error reported by IBSYS. Wilson or I had programmed a powerful error recovery algorithm into our own system's original 1301 code, so I looked at the I/O error log in our own system to see if our system had a problem similar to IBSYS's. It showed that we had recovered from many such errors.

With help from our log data, Roger pinned the error down to the electro-magnetic coil in the actuator assembly. He immediately ordered a replacement and learned that it would take a couple days to receive it. Operations personnel were in a quandary. It seemed that the only solution was to go back to using the tape-based systems (IBSYS at least) until the disk drive was fixed.

Roger came to the rescue by engineering a temporary fix. He calculated how much current on that size wire might fuse the break together (or melt it completely). Then he figured what size capacitor would hold the right charge at a voltage he also calculated. His experiment would fail if the junction of broken wire melted rather than welded, but there was nothing to lose. When he finally connected the charged capacitor across the coil terminals, his scheme worked! The 1301 ran fine for three days before Roger's weld let go. By then the new actuator assembly had arrived. Roger installed it while our systems ran, oh so slowly, off tape-based systems for a few hours.

"Cleaning" the IBM 1301

For about three years, circa 1964–66, a second 7094 was installed to process data for a special project. When the project ended, the lease on its 7094 did also. Other than associating with the programmers of that computer, I had nothing to do with it until the day before the lease expired.

On the day before the computer system was due to be moved out, someone noted that the 1301 disk—with much classified data—had not been erased. Then, as now, files were "deleted" by clearing the directory entry that pointed to the data and freeing the space occupied by the file. The data would not be destroyed until it was overwritten by other data. The programmer in charge mistakenly thought he had erased the data, but had merely "deleted" it. Those folks had absolutely no idea of how to systematically erase the data.

I was called to the computer room late that afternoon and briefed on their dilemma. They had 20 hours—until noon the next day—to "triple wipe" all the disk surfaces, that is, to write random numbers throughout the drive three times before releasing it, per directives from the Pentagon.

At that point, their lack of planning became an emergency on my part. Wilson and I were the only two local programmers familiar with writing machine-level code for the 1301. We had provided higher-level interfaces for all the others. I was charged with writing and executing a program to triple-erase the 1301 before the next noon.

I do not remember whether or not I went home that night. It took several hours to find a random number generator. By the next morning I had coded the program, had it keypunched, assembled it, and debugged it. About 7 or 8 o'clock in the morning, my program started wiping the disks. I thought it would be done in an hour or two. As I recall, it finished about noon, just in the nick of time.

A couple people's necks had just been saved. Neither of them ever told me, "Thanks." That's life!

The IBM 1405

IBM's 1405 Disk Storage Unit was announced in 1961 for use with the IBM 1401 computer. It could have two modules, with fifty recording surfaces per module on 25 large disks, containing a total of ten million characters per module. It had a single read/write head on an access mechanism that traveled up and down, in and out.

The IBM 1311 and 2311

The 1311, IBM's last disk product before advent of the S/360 (IBM System/360) computers, was announced in October 1962 for various existing computers, and had the first removable disks. Its IBM 1316 disk pack had six 14-inch diameter disks and weighed about ten pounds. There was a read/write head for each of the ten recording surfaces on a single hydraulic actuator. It had a capacity of 2MB. The 1311 came in seven models for three groups of pre-S/360 computers.

The 2311 was introduced in 1964 for the S/360 family. Its design came from its predecessor, the 1311, but it had 200 tracks per surface versus 100 on the 1311. That and other improvements yielded a capacity of over 7MB. The access mechanism was similar to that of the 1311.

Start-Up Competitors

The 2311 was made with a standard interface for the entire S/360 computer family. That helped start-up companies to spring up all over the Santa Clara Valley (around San Jose, where IBM's 2311 manufacturing operation was located). I saw their advertisements in the trade press. The procedure would be to buy 2311s from IBM, reverse-engineer them, and duplicate the parts, buying some from IBM's own vendors when possible.

Such a company could advertise plug-compatible equivalents for much less than IBM had to charge, having done all the research and development. One company even had the audacity to advertise that its disk drive was identical to IBM's except for the covers. (That ad soon disappeared.)

A small company faced with such unfair competition could file suit for the patent violator to cease, desist, and pay a penalty. Such suits are much less likely to succeed when the plaintiff has a large market share, even in the case of multiple patent violations.

The parts, of course, were useless without engineering and manufacturing expertise. After I went to work for IBM, I was contacted by at least one headhunter, trying to "buy me away." Other local IBMers were contacted as well. Most of us had enough loyalty and security at IBM to resist such offers. There was also the risk of the new company not becoming viable. There were other reasons not to take the bait, but some did. One of my engineering counterparts was enticed to leave IBM because of a start-up company's ridiculously high pay offer. We met in a store one day a few months later and I asked him how he was doing. He was on salary, with no money for overtime, and had been working 70-hour weeks, month after month. His marriage was on the rocks. He hardly knew his own kids anymore. He had burned his IBM bridge behind him when he went to work for a competitor.

The IBM 2314 and 2319

The 2314 was announced in April 1965, a year after the S/360 announcement. Model 1 consisted of a row of five cabinets containing nine removable disk packs—eight active drives and a spare, each with a capacity approaching 30MB—at one fourth the cost of data on the 2311. The data rate was over 310,000 bytes/second—twice that of the 2311. Models A1, A2, and B1 followed with various configurations and modest improvements. The 2319 could be added to a 2314 to provide more drives. Both the 2314 and the 2319 used the IBM 2316 disk pack, which had twice the recording surfaces (20, on 11 disks) as the 1316.

I was involved with manufacturing automation for the 2314 (see Sorting Magnetic Heads in the COMATS section).

IBM 2314

The IBM 3330, 3340, 3350, 3370, 3380, and 3390

I set up a test data transmission scheme at IBM's San Jose manufacturing facility for final test of the control unit of a product (known as Merlin at the time) which was introduced in June 1970 as the IBM 3330. It more than tripled the capacity of its predecessor, the 2314. The disk packs for early model 3330s each held 100MB, and the Model 11 doubled that. 3330s were developed for use in the new System/370s, named for the decade of the '70s (which were compatible with their older brothers, the S/360s).

My successor(s) did the same as above for the *Winchester*, or IBM 3340, about three years later, and *Madrid* (3350) about 1975. The disk packs for these units contained the head/access arm assembly. Each 3350 unit in a string (of up to 8 units) could hold over 300MB.

By the time the IBM 3370 (later '70s), 3380 (in 1980), and 3390 came along, I had moved from plant floor automation to the Product Test Laboratory, working with ultra-high-speed printers. In fact, within 3 months of the 3380 announcement, I had been moved to IBM's Tucson, Arizona plant. Capacities had broken the gigabyte barrier, transmission rates had passed the MB-per-second mark, and cost was below $50 per MB. or about three orders of magnitude below their earliest ancestors.

We could not imagine, in the 1970s, that by 2010, we could buy a 2 terabyte disk drive for around $100. What was furthest from our minds was that, by 2007, rotating storage would be in the process of being replaced by solid-state storage devices of even greater capacities for lower costs. Will hard disks be the latest dinosaurs of the computer age?

Some Early Terminals

The Teletype

With the invention of the telegraph and Morse code in the 1800s, messages and data could be transmitted "quickly," compared to ordinary mail. A human was needed to key in the code at the sending end of the wire. One might say that the Morse code key was the world's first terminal, simple as it was. Another person was needed at the receiving end to translate the *dits* and *dahs* into characters, words, and sentences.

If the Morse code key was the first terminal, I would say that the teletype was next. The creation of machines to automate the translations of characters to code, and code to characters started in 1902. The latter machine would be called a telegraphic typewriter, or *teletype*.

In 1910 a machine was created that would both send and receive. A series of continuously improved machines followed. In the mid-1920s, the Teletype Corporation was founded. About 1930 they joined American Telephone & Telegraph (AT&T).

In the decades of the 1930s, '40s, and '50s, speeds increased in various increments from 50 words per minute to 300 words per minute.

In the 1950s, IBM worked with the U.S. Air Force to create the *Semi-Automatic Ground Environment*, or SAGE system, using computers and teletype machines to link the people operating the North American Aerospace Defense Command (NORAD).

Teletype machines were also in the early thinking (1957) of a joint effort of American Airlines and IBM to create a computerized reservation system. The project was named SABER, and later renamed to SABRE (*Semi-Automated Business Research Environment*). It was tested initially in 1960 and was doing all of American's booking of seats by 1964. SABRE stretched the state of the art in specially-modified 7090 computers and specially-designed terminals. IBM was said to have extended many lessons from SABRE into design of the S/360.

The IBM 1030 and 1050

In 1967 I encountered two terminal types on pedestals at IBM. One was an input terminal, the IBM 1030 Data Collection System, and the other (for output) was the IBM 1050 Data Communications System. They were made for short transactions by people standing up.

The San Jose IBM manufacturing plant used a number of the input terminals for labor claiming. Workers would insert their badge, which had pre-punched holes to identify them, into one slot. Then they would insert an IBM card into another slot. The punches in the card would identify a job and the tasks performed. Then they would set several sliders, each with ten positions to specify a decimal digit, to indicate a quantity, such as pieces produced or a number of hours and tenths.

There was no dialog between system and terminal operator—and therefore no error checking. Whatever was input, good data or bad, went into the system, a phenomenon known in the industry as *Garbage in/Garbage out,* or *GIGO.* A corresponding output terminal based on an electric typewriter could be installed and, had it been used, it could have provided somewhat of a feedback loop for error-checking.

In the early 1970s I led a group of three who reprogrammed the previous application to use touch-tone phones to replace the error-prone one-way setup. Our computer had an audio response unit attached, which had 128 often-used words on a spinning drum. Each word was at a particular drum address. Our program could pick a set of addresses of the words for its response to a terminal operator and put the words onto that operator's phone line in a monotone, saying that the transaction was okay or describing the error, in which case the operator would retry. That technology has come a long way since then!

The IBM 2741

The IBM 2741 was a heavy-duty Selectric typewriter terminal. I used one in 1975 to compose a document of about a dozen pages. The 2741 could not back up in the document to make insertions on earlier pages, so I had to close the file and reopen it, starting again at the beginning. Then I would have it retype everything down to my insertion or correction point. That was better than any other tool I had at my disposal.

Ordinarily I would have used a shared pool of secretaries, who normally typed all our (usually handwritten) documents on Selectric typewriters with removable memory devices. If we were lucky, we would get our typed document in a day or two. The urgency of my particular task did not allow a long wait. I worked late into the evening, finishing my document so it was ready to copy and distribute the next morning.

IBM 2260 Video Display Terminal

A 2260's human interface consisted of a cathode ray display tube and a keyboard. The tube could display information being typed in, information from the mainframe computer, or a combination of both. We supported them extensively on the plant floor, as noted below. They were plain but powerful, compared to anything we had previously.

Imagine my son Chuck's astonishment at an IBM open house day with the IBM 2260 CRT terminal on the desk in my office. Contrary to a teletype terminal which was all he had ever known, the 2260's screen displayed the entire context around the current point of entry, signified by the cursor symbol, like the ones we have on our screens today. One could insert, delete, copy, and paste entire sections of text. Today we take this for granted, but at that time it was a big deal to Chuck, who had never had that flexibility. Someone from today would not know why this is a big deal–they could not imagine his astonishment. This was the beginning of networking, and a totally new concept in an industry that had relied on punched cards.

IBM 3270 Video Display Terminal

In 1976, when I transferred to the Product Test Laboratory, I met my first 3270, a successor to the 2260 with several new features. The 3270s were with us still at my retirement in 1992. When we began to use personal computers as terminals in the early 1980s, we used emulator programs to make them look like 3270s to the big mainframe computer.

Chapter 10: The IBM System 360

In April of 1964, IBM announced the System/360. As an employee of a customer of IBM, the Navy's Pacific Missile Range, I had been serving on the Input/Output Committee of SHARE for almost three years. I/O Committee members had signed nondisclosure agreements with IBM before starting to evaluate the specifications of the I/O subsystems of OS/360, the operating system for System/360. This started for me a year or so before the announcement. The sophistication of the I/O services spelled out in the specifications was an order of magnitude above anything we had previously seen in the industry.

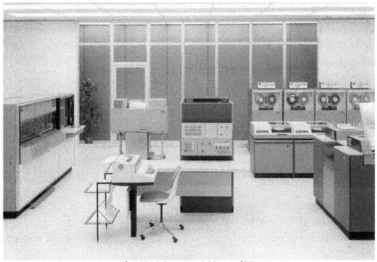

The IBM System 360-mod25

The System/360 started a great revolution in computing. It was a computer family that would serve both scientific and commercial applications, and that could grow with a business.

Scientific vs. Commercial

Until S/360 appeared, a given computer was either scientific or commercial, but not both. A scientific computer worked with binary integers and floating-point numbers. Conversion of the fractional part of a binary number to a decimal format incurs a *round off* error, because the values of powers of two do not coincide with any of the values of powers of ten. As a result, $30,000.00 might print as $29,999.99, which would be completely unacceptable in the world of finance.

Conversely, commercial machines represented numbers in a binary-coded decimal format, which worked fine for dollars and cents but was intolerable for scientific calculations. The cousin of the old IBM 709 scientific computer was the IBM 705 decimal computer. The 709 was unsatisfactory for decimal calculations, just as the 705 was unsatisfactory for scientific calculations. Other computer manufacturers and their customers were faced with the same problem.

Finding the Solution

The number of successive computers in each of several diverse lines from IBM, just one of several computer manufacturers in the 1950s, became overwhelming. Parallel lines became a serious problem in the industry.

By 1961 it had become apparent to IBM that it could no longer afford to produce two or more parallel lines of computers. The Seven Dwarfs together threatened IBM's market share. None of the strategic proposals put forth within the company provided a solution to IBM's woes, so the company turned to a method that had often solved similar problems in the past. The leaders assembled a secret Task Force of 13 highly-talented independent thinkers, sent them to a motel with private conference facilities, and told them not to come back without a solution.

The task force was code-named SPREAD, for Systems Programming REsearch And Development, and it operated in strict secrecy for two months. The team had top-priority access to any company resources they needed. I said that they were independent thinkers. In some ways, it would be similar to pitting a number of Democrats against the same number of Republicans in Congress. Some of their design ideas and theories were diametrically opposed to each other. The big difference is that they were not allowed to fail. Three days before the end of 1961, SPREAD released its comprehensive report that contained the solution: the S/360.

The Solution

S/360's basic architecture was binary, but it included decimal number support as an option, including circuitry and instructions for decimal number representations and calculations. It was done by encoding each decimal digit into 4 binary bits. I never saw an S/360 without the decimal option.

Just as important, a customer could start with a smaller computer and graduate to a compatible larger model of S/360 when needed. Today we take that for granted, but before the advent of S/360 it was not possible. Prior to that, nearly all programs had to be rewritten from scratch when a company bought a more powerful machine. Most programs were written either in an assembler language for a particular computer, or in a compiler language that may or may not be easily transportable to another specific computer.

Betting the Company

As development of S/360 progressed, it demanded more and more company resources. Six compatible computers of varying degrees of power and cost were being designed in IBM's laboratories in several locations, including England. The most expensive model would have fifty times the power of the least expensive one. The SPREAD specifications were remarkable in that those six models could all run the same programs, limited only by such things as memory size and peripheral devices.

The operating system software was named OS/360. Development of OS/360 was the largest programming project ever attempted in the world until then. IBM hired experienced programmers and trained new ones in staggering numbers.

The development of S/360 and its OS/360 software was a monumental effort, requiring the whole of the largest computer manufacturer in the world to pull it off.

A year or two after the 1964 S/360 announcement, I was told that when IBM found itself over-committed, the buck passed to Chairman and CEO Tom Watson, Jr. about slipping schedules and the shortage of developers. After some deliberation, he pulled the plug on all fallback plans, devoting all of IBM to S/360. He "bet the company" on S/360. Had it failed, IBM would have been eaten alive by its competition.

Tom Watson, Jr.

I had the privilege of working for IBM while "TJ" was still in charge of the company founded by his dad. The Watsons were not bureaucrats, and betting the company on that one highly promising product was not a surprising thing for him to do.

Tom Watson, Jr. with the IBM 1620

I want to copy a memo here that he wrote to all employees:

"Let's avoid being overly cautious, conservative, playing it safe. We should have the courage to take risks when they are thoughtful risks. We must try to make clear, sound, aggressive decisions, not waiting until every possible base has been touched. Each of us must aim to make his own decisions and shun the process of decision by agreement of all possible interested parties. We should be motivated by what is right for the IBM Company rather than by the niceties of internal diplomacy. We expect that there will be mistakes. We must forgive mistakes which have been made because someone was trying to act aggressively in the Company's interest."

T. J. Watson, Jr., 12/25/57

I deeply respected the Watsons. Their company was founded on respect for the individual and their company treated us that way. On the other hand, one who didn't care to help the Company could be fired awfully fast. After TJ retired, some of those principles were watered down. Finally, during IBM's crises in the mid-1980s and the 1990s, all pretenses were removed by new company leaders. Their decisions were predicated much more by raw dollars. Perhaps that was needed for IBM to survive, but to many of us it was the unfortunate passing of a way of working life.

One of the stories—legend or true—about Tom Watson, Sr. had to do with a million-dollar mistake by one of his top executives. After working at home one night to write his resignation letter and trying to prepare his family for his unemployment, the distraught manager was called into "the old man's" office the next morning, and he offered his letter of resignation.

"Resign?" roared Mr. Watson, "I just spent a million dollars on your education, and you want to resign?"

If you want to read about two fascinating men, the Watsons, read *Father, Son, & Co.* by Tom Watson, Jr. and Peter Petre. TJ states that he was a brat as a boy and backs it up with his own stories. As a young man, he manipulated the system to become a civilian pilot, then an Army Air Corps pilot in World War II. After the war, he rose to the top of the world's largest computer manufacturer, retired, and became U.S. Ambassador to Russia. As incongruous as it sounds, it all ties together.

The Announcement

There are two ways to get a product ready for market. One way is to keep it secret from the competition. The other is to file a patent application, so that your competition can't use it without your permission.

In filing a patent application, the applicant's design becomes public from that moment on. Even though others cannot use it without a license, they can prepare reactive strategies.

IBM often depended upon trade secrets to preserve its rights until just the right time to file for a patent. On April 6, 1964, the IBM Corporation filed patent applications for its S/360 and numerous unique components.

On the next day, April 7, it used movies to announce the S/360 and OS/360 to its potential customers and the media through exclusive parties held in key cities around the world.

Microsoft and others seem to have taken that idea and expanded it with modern technology in modern-day announcements.

An important new computer announcement by Snow White had been anticipated by the Seven Dwarfs. Rumors were rife in the trade press. IBM's competitors had tried to prepare for it with various contingent announcements of their own to follow.

The trade secrets had been well-kept, right up until the patent filings. On April 7, 1964 the competition was blown away, so to speak. A machine that could handle both scientific and commercial applications? Six sizes? Relocatable programs? As if that were not enough, another 150 features and peripheral products were also announced at the same time. It was enough to boggle anyone's mind! OS/360, whose software concepts went well beyond most people's imaginations, added even more fuel to the fire.

IBM had some experience with converting the old tape-based IBSYS for the 709x to run on the 1301 disk drive. OS/360 was disk-based from the start, using the new 2311 disk drives. Not only did OS/360 reside on disk, but new access methods allowed writing and reading data files on disk.

I was still a Civil Service employee of the Navy. I would not have wanted to be working for one of IBM's competitors on that day!

Shipment of the first S/360, the model 40, was a year away, as was OS/360. It was a time for orders. Preparation would need that year or more.

IBM was inundated with a problem most companies would envy: more orders than marketing had projected or that manufacturing was prepared to handle. IBM was still catching up on backlogs three years later when I went to work for them. TJ's "bet the company" decision not only paid off, but it revolutionized the industry. Other computer manufacturers scrambled to follow suit.

Software Conversion

Although a solution to the problem of transportability of programs was on the horizon, it was not yet solved. The hurdle was the conversion of countless programs, written for other hardware, to run on S/360. Many programs in existence had been written in assembler language for a specific machine. S/360 had a totally different instruction set and a different architecture from any other existing computer. Even COBOL and FORTRAN programs needed some modifications.

An astronomical effort to rewrite many of the nation's programs to run on S/360 was soon underway by many customers at great cost, creating an acute shortage of programmers and leading to their extensive job-hopping for several years.

Multiprogramming

It had become clear that a computer could keep up with several users at once, if only each could have a turn every few milliseconds. The computer would also have time to do some other tasks at a lower priority in the background. For example, between each keystroke that I make while writing this book, the computer has plenty of spare time to send part of a document to the printer and work on some other tasks too. I might have to wait for a few milliseconds—so short a time that I would not even know I was waiting.

The advent of S/360 and its competitors brought about *multiprogramming*, or *multitasking*, the practice of having more than one application at a time taking turns at running in one computer. If you are talking on the phone while cooking dinner, you are multitasking.

Another way of thinking of multitasking is to visualize two or more programs concurrently loaded into a computer and taking turns running. While one is waiting for a record to be read or written, another can process data that it already has, and vice-versa.

Multiprogramming had been barely possible but not practical on the 709x and comparable computers. First, it was not practical without a fast way to save, and later restore, the state of each program as they took turns being executed. Second, it was impractical in most instances without the benefit of program relocatability. Finally, high-speed memory was very limited. It was hard enough for the operating system and *one* program to fit. S/360 was designed to solve those problems, at least enough to make multitasking practical.

Time-Sharing

If a computer had the ability to run more than one program concurrently, the next step was to provide the means for different people to communicate with their own application programs (tasks) in *real-time* through terminal devices, by sharing the computer's time. Think of the keyboard and display on your home computer as a terminal.

Programs could be designed to follow a "gentlemen's agreement" to yield control while waiting for I/O, thus allowing the next program in line to run, and so on. A few programmers ignored the agreement, causing bottlenecks. One solution was for operating systems to gain such control automatically though I/O utilities used by the programs.

Programs can be divided into two classes, *Input/Output-bound* or *execute-bound*. I/O-bound programs spend most of their time waiting for data to be read or written. An execute-bound program spends most of its time computing. It is also known as a *number cruncher*.

When an execute-bound program gained control, it had a tendency to hog the system, to the chagrin of those with I/O-bound applications. The solution was for the operating system to set a timer each time it gave control to an application program. If the program had not relinquished control before the timer expired, the system would forcibly take control and pass it to the next program in line.

Time-sharing systems became prevalent in the later 1960s and early 1970s. With the development of various devices designed as computer terminals, time-sharing system offerings became very popular. I used a time-sharing system and the BASIC language for a project in 1967. BASIC (Beginner's All-purpose Symbolic Instruction Code) was developed by John Kemeny and Thomas Kurtz at Dartmouth College in 1964, and was quite popular because it was an easy-to-learn, friendly language.

Our eldest son, Chuck, attending a parochial high school in the first half of the 1970s, became proficient on a time-sharing system. His access was through that school's teletype terminal, which was connected to the "great computer in the sky" through an acoustic modem and a phone line. Two students—Chuck and his buddy—actually taught some of their teachers how to use the time-share terminal.

Operating Systems for System/360

OS/360

The first version of an S/360 operating system was released in 1965, a year after announcement, and was known simply as OS/360, Release 1. It represented a giant leap of sophistication over any previous operating system in the world.

The smaller machines did not have the capacity to run OS/360. They utilized either a subset called PCP (Principal Control Program, 1966) or DOS (not to be confused with PC-DOS for the personal computer 15 years later). The following gives a rough idea of advances in DOS:

- DOS (1966) Disk Operating System
- DOS-2314 (1967) 2314 was a removable media disk drive
- DOS-MP (1968) Multiprogramming
- DOS/VS (1973) Virtual Storage

For the larger machines, within ten years of the announcement in 1964, the following variants (and others) had been created[1]. For less formal designations of the names below, either the prefix OS/360 or just the 360 is often omitted, for example: MVT or OS/MVT.

- OS/360-MFT (1967) Multiprogramming with a Fixed number of Tasks
- OS/360-MVT (1967–8) Multiprogramming with a Variable number of Tasks
- OS/360-MFT II (1968)
- OS/360-TSO (1971) Time Sharing Option
- OS/360-SVS (1972) Single Virtual Storage
- OS/360-VS1 (1972) OS/MFT with Virtual Storage
- OS/360-VS2, OS/MVT with virtual storage, which grew into SVS and MVS (1974) Multiple Virtual Storage. MVS was the typical progenitor of more advanced systems created in the latter 1970s, the '80s, and the '90s.

Some of these variants of OS/360 were developed for certain specialized functions, such as TSO (Time Sharing Option), or for certain kinds of hardware configurations. TSO actually had a predecessor, TSS (Time Sharing System). In its attempt to

---

1   *IBM Journal of Research and Development,* Vol. 25, No.5, September 1981; pp.471-82

be all things to all users, TSS was not only painfully inefficient but usually crashed in less time after IPL than it had taken to IPL, and was finally abandoned. TSO was somewhat inefficient and a space hog, and its user base, after IBM began to license VM to customers (see below), shrunk dramatically.

A constant theme of these systems is their compatibility, so that a user could graduate to a later system without significant retrofitting.

Just to describe all the significant features of each of the systems listed above is beyond the scope of this publication. Suffice it to say that the continuous trend since the 1950s has been to automate more and more actions, gradually releasing the mainframe's operator and the user from tedious procedures and decisions, and giving the user more direct power with less (or no) operator intervention.

VM: The Virtual Machine Facility

An operating system was desired that would create a virtual machine (computer) for each user. Early work in that regard led to several efforts that failed, before advent of the successful VM/370 in 1972 in IBM's research center at MIT. VM's control program (CP) allowed numerous users, each with a virtual computer, to develop and test their applications independently. Each user (at a terminal) was provided the appearance of a dedicated computer. Many users switched from running under TSO, to running the more efficient MVT or MVS under VM.

Within IBM, VM became the overwhelming favorite for various functions, particularly development and test of any code—from an application program to a complete operating system. With pressure from its customers for several years, IBM finally licensed VM to them. The number of those licenses grew into tens of thousands.

On later versions of VM, systems programmers could develop and test new or modified operating systems on their own virtual computers under control of CP. Even further, it could be used to test a new or existing operating system on a virtual image of hardware being developed but not yet in existence. Indeed, it was also used to test new versions of VM under VM. One example of a VM application is in the HEX Testing section, later in the book.

Does the 360 live on?

In mid-1970 IBM announced the System/370, successor to the System/360, with virtual hardware, an improved instruction set, and various other enhancements, then or later, such as extended addressing. Also, it was upward compatible. Programs that ran on the S/360 could also run on the S/370.

The IBM Enterprise Systems Architecture/390, more commonly called ESA/390, System/390 or S/390, was introduced in 1990. Various improvements, such as fiber-optic cables, new CPU technology, much smaller main-frames, and other changes took place in six stages, or generations, right up through 1999.

The IBM eServer zSeries succeeded the S/390 in the year 2000. A program written for the S/360 in 1964 would still run on an eServer in the next century. On May 13, 2003, Wilson Cooper, my past technical boss and co-worker from the 1960s, sent me the following email message: "Does the 360 live on? Today's Wall Street Journal Marketplace section headlines, 'Rare Bright Spot in Tech—IBM Mainframes.' The article describes the x990 eServer, codenamed T-Rex, that is 'the latest generation of a product that turned IBM into a corporate dynamo after its unveiling in 1964.'"[2]

Mentioning the name of a server, above, raises the question of what a server is. A server does just what it says. It serves other computers by connecting them together in networks.

Networks

The Advanced Research Projects Agency (ARPA) of the U.S. Defense Department, early in the 1960s, had a need to link several computers so that they could communicate with each other. What they created was the first computer network, ARPAnet. It was followed by two successful but mutually incompatible networks, each with its own unique benefits.

ARPA's new challenge was to enable those networks (and many more, as it turned out), now called *intranets*, to directly interact. To do this a linkage method was invented with protocols, or rules, for transmission of data between networks. It was named the *Internet*, and life was never going to be the same. The two most important protocols were the *Transmission Control Protocol* (TCP) and the *Internet Protocol* (IP). The entire set of protocols was named *TCP/IP*. Through most of the decade of the 1980s the Internet grew while restricted to specific agencies.

Ethernet, one of the most popular local area networks was developed in the 1970s at PARC[3], the Palo Alto Research Center,.

In the 1970s many companies, especially larger ones, created their own *local area networks* (LANs) and *wide area networks* (WANs). TCP/IP was the most widely

2   *Wall Street Journal.* (Eastern edition) New York, N.Y.: May 13, 2003. pg. B.1

3   PARC is discussed in the Graphical User Interfaces section later on.

used protocol. For example, in the late 1970s a number of IBM plants each created a local area network, which were soon linked to create the IBM worldwide net. In the '80s, quite a few of my peers seemed to spend an inordinate amount of time on the IBM net, *surfing*, as we would say today, or participating in forums. It was a temptation that I could not afford much time to indulge.

In the late 1980s, restrictions on use of the Internet were eased. Many commercial networks connected to it, and many more were created. They grew at an astounding rate and that is expected to continue into the foreseeable future.

There are a number of Internet problems to be resolved in the future. Perhaps the primary one is to devise a way of increasing capacity to handle the expanding flow of data. There are numerous proposals and works in progress to resolve this and other problems.

Chapter 11: Life at IBM

COMATS

Three months after being hired by IBM in 1967, I transferred to the Manufacturing Engineering organization. Within ME was a group of three departments totaling about 45 workers. The group was named COMATS, after the system its people had created a year or two before my arrival—the *Computer-Oriented Manufacturing and Test System*. Their goals were to solve a problem of data logistics (having the right control data at the right place at the right time) and to save money on computer memory, which was still very expensive by today's standards.

One department dealt with the hardware. I was in one of the two software departments. We all worked very much in conjunction with each other. I arrived in time to help COMATS spread through numerous manufacturing operations over a nine year period.

Disk memory costs in those days were on the order of a thousand dollars per megabyte. Machine-control data, in the volume needed, took many, many megabytes. So my predecessors (who became my teammates) at IBM San Jose devised COMATS, composed of many small computers, each linked to a mainframe computer. The small computers had no secondary memory, such as disks or tapes. The engineers installed special circuits so that they could even use their links to the host for booting up.

Numerous machines that automated manufacturing and testing on the manufacturing floor were each controlled by one of these small computers whose brains were "upstairs" at the mainframe, so to speak.

Shortly after I arrived, we moved COMATS from an IBM 1460 to twin S/360 Model 40 mainframes which mirrored each other so that if one failed, the other would continue to communicate with the various manufacturing areas. They each had 256K of high speed memory.

Our S/360s also had a teleprocessing network. Our online programs, whether written to "talk" to satellite computers or TP terminals, were each limited to 4 kilobytes. Only a few of them could run concurrently, so our systems programmer imposed an automatic time limit for any one program to occupy memory.

We wrote programs for the mainframe to communicate with production workers through our teleprocessing network of about a hundred IBM 2260 terminals.

What we could *not* do was use 2260s to write our programs. We could not write our online programs online. We were a little ahead of the times. Our model 40s were dedicated to online applications. We had to do all of our assemblies on a larger computer run by other departments. They lacked the storage capacity to store source code for online compilers and assemblers. Our expertise rubbed off on them after a while, and storage grew less expensive, but in the meantime, all our assemblies were from card decks. The procedure was similar to the one described earlier in the *Computer Room Procedures* section, except ten years later and in a different organization.

You may have noticed I said *assemblies*. Our code had to be tight, so we wrote our programs in S/360 assembler language. We could not use compilers, except for report programs that were to run as background (batch) jobs at a lower priority level.

To review a bit, wired to the twin mainframes were two networks. One network consisted of up to 255 coaxial cable connections to small satellite computers in the various manufacturing areas in the plant (what we called *the plant floor*). The other network was a teleprocessing net, mostly connected to IBM 2260 terminals. So, the first net was connected to satellite computers, while the teleprocessing net connected to people using terminals. Most of those people were operating the satellite computers. There were generally both types of connection—satellites and people—to any given manufacturing area on the plant floor.

We looked for a teleprocessing subsystem under OS/360, but those available at that time were not adequate for some of our special needs, so a couple of our programmers created a teleprocessing subsystem for us. We converted numerous batch applications to run online through the 2260s. These speeded up the plant floor operations for those applications and, therefore, speeded up production.

One of our TP system maintenance programmers had not learned the lesson that, even for a small change, one had to do a thorough test. Indeed, testing could consume 90% of the total effort in some cases. If his test system was released to production mode too soon, a thousand people could suddenly be idled when it crashed. This happened one time too many, and we didn't see him anymore.

After this overall introduction, the following stories might help the reader to understand what COMATS was all about on a day-to-day basis.

Sorting Magnetic Heads

For several months I was loaned another programmer for a project to classify newly-made magnetic recording heads (for IBM 2314 disk drives) according to seven electro-magnetic measurements. There were hundreds of combinations, far too many for humans to sort accurately. Our program (on an old IBM 1710 decimal computer connected to the COMATS server) analyzed those measurements and designated each head as *good* (use it), *bad* (scrap it), or *rework* (fix it). Its star feature was to accurately designate one of about three dozen rework procedures to be performed to salvage a marginal head. This does not sound very important until one learns that about $1000 was already invested in each head. Once our program was in production, it didn't take long to save IBM a million dollars.

Making Printed Circuit Boards

Another project I spent a year or so on, as a maintenance programmer, was the *board line*, which used computer-driven data to create printed circuit boards. To make just a few unique boards economically, a machine called a *printed circuit generator* traced a narrow beam of light upon a board's photosensitive surface in a dark room. The beam was controlled by computer commands that turned it on and off at appropriate points and gave it X and Y coordinates to travel. Hundreds of circuits, each just a few thousandths of an inch wide, could be traced in a few minutes—a task that a human would not even try. Then, through a chemical bath, the circuits were developed and the non-exposed material etched away.

Our circuit boards were complex and crowded. I never saw a board that did not also require thin yellow circuit wires to be installed between predetermined connecting pins, supplementing the printed "wires" when there was no space for more. We had another machine for that, called the *wire-wrap machine*, or the *Gardner-Denver*, after the company that made it. It would, by computer control, install yellow wires of the required lengths between specified pairs of pins on a board.

Yet another machine, the *printed circuit tester* (PCT), performed hundreds of thousands of tests for errors—open and closed circuits—also in a few minutes and under computer control. Someone once told me (they had done some arithmetic) that it would take a person three work weeks of eight-hour days, focusing completely on the task and not making a single mistake, to do what the PCT did in fifteen minutes. (On top of that, the PCT never had to take a break or go to the restroom.)

Each Board Line machine was controlled by its own satellite computer that downloaded the data necessary for the task at hand from the mainframe.

The Engineering Change Machine

My partner Larry and I mostly just maintained previously-written programs that generated control data for the machines above, but we once hurriedly created a set of programs to generate data for yet another behemoth, called the *engineering change machine.*

Engineering changes, or E/Cs, are very common on electronic circuit boards. E/Cs take place throughout manufacturing cycles, especially early in those cycles, to fix design errors, to simplify circuits, or to add new features. It is inevitable that some boards with the old design have to be scrapped due to instant obsolescence (a significant loss), unless they can be modified.

Enter the E/C machine. One of our engineer counterparts, an "internal customer" of ours, if you wish, actually found a loophole to purchase it with IBM dollars. Then he discovered there were no programs to create control data for it to modify IBM's boards (he was a true "wild duck"[1]). Our manager could have used the old quote: "A lack of planning on your part does not constitute an emergency on ours," but for the good of the company he gave Larry and me the green light to borrow a third programmer for a couple months, and our programs successfully generated control data for the E/C machine after we fixed our share of bugs.

The E/C machine had three modes of operation, and on a given board they went in this sequence:

1. Remove yellow wires from specified connection points. This was done with a tool that unwrapped the wire's ends from around their two pins.
2. Delete specified printed circuits, using a hollow circular cutter that descended around specified pins, in turn, and spun to cut the printed circuit connections at the pins.

---

1 Wild Duck: a moniker applied by past IBM Chairman Tom Watson, Jr. to those who can move a project quickly by cutting through red tape and excessive procedures. Watson felt that there was a place for wild ducks in a company like IBM, one that tended, by its very size, to be somewhat bureaucratic. Also, refer to Watson, Jr's memo on bureaucracy under his heading in the S/360 chapter.

3. Add yellow wires (of the right length) between specified pins. The tool spun the stripped ends of a wire around the pins.

Imagine our consternation, during the first live test (on a scrap board), when the machine selected the *printed circuit delete* tool and tried to delete a printed circuit that was buried under a yellow wire. The program was supposed to have removed the wire first. After a few more such disasters, we finally fixed our last known bug, and the E/C machine started its illustrious career of saving boards from the scrap heap.

A few months later, our manager put the Board Line back into Larry's hands and put me in the area of data control at the mainframe, where I spent the next year or two writing new programs.

A worker would enter a transaction through a 2260 terminal that would ask the host computer for the appropriate program which, in turn, would find the right control data for a specific board type and ship it down to the nearby satellite computer's high speed memory—its only memory.

My first new task was to write an online TP transaction processor to receive a request from the plant floor and automatically call for my other new program to be loaded and send test data over a coaxial cable to a particular satellite computer. That satellite was the new tester for the Merlin control unit (the IBM 3330 disk drive) that was soon to go into production. One thing led to another. I wrote a number of such programs.

Moving Systems between Plants

I next worked on a project to copy IBM's *circuit card manufacturing* production line in Endicott, New York, and install it on the west coast (San Jose) as a supplemental source of cards. (*Cards* have circuit components on them, and several of them plug into one *board*.)

Two others and I had responsibility for learning and cloning the computer systems and application programs and getting them to run in San Jose.

In conjunction with that, we were directed to also create a Defect Reporting system, so Tom, an engineer-turned-programmer, got to write his first official program, which would collect defect data online. The Defect Reporting system would focus manufacturing management's attention, on a daily basis, on the previous day's ten worst production problems for each department, from two standpoints: quantities wasted and dollars lost.

Our little system worked great! It collected data online and, at midnight, it "closed the books" for the previous 24-hour day. A timer was set on the mainframe to call programs after midnight to process and analyze problems, and produce reports of the previous day's worst problems. When the department managers arrived at work in the morning, the reports were on their desks. At that point, the proverbial monkey was on their backs.

A year or so later I was tapped to help move yet another manufacturing line (from the IBM plant near Boulder, Colorado) to San Jose. Most of it was cut and dried, once I arrived there and figured it out. The major challenge was an online quality control application written in S/360 Assembler Language. It had to be modified for the San Jose environment. My manager gave me a middle-aged programmer with many years' experience, exclusively with PL/1 (compiler) programs, so my challenge was to make him productive in Assembler quickly, while still getting my primary work done.

Well, we were keeping our heads above water, or at least our mouths. We were almost done when I was scheduled for an operation (not work related). At that point I was helping him learn to analyze memory dumps of his crashed program. I hoped he would be able to finish it on his own when I left work the night before my operation.

I reported to the hospital on schedule the next morning. I awoke in the recovery room about mid-day. A nurse wheeled me to my ward, my temporary home for the next couple days. I had told my partner to call if he had a question that I might be able to answer over the phone. I was still groggy from the anesthesia and was glad he didn't call until the next morning. His program had crashed and he had a memory dump. After a few minutes of questions over the phone, it became obvious that I'd have to look at it to help him, so he came to see me at the hospital.

When the nurse walked in, there I was with a three-hundred-page stack of fan-folded paper on my lap in bed, with paperclips attached here and there as page markers. If you've never seen an OS/360 dump, it was on 11 x 14-inch paper and was mostly covered with millions of hexadecimal numbers comprising the operating system, programs, and data. The nurse took one look and shook her head in resignation. We found the problem, he fixed it, and I went through the whole rest of my recovery weeks without another call from him.

Moving Pains

My manager wanted to cut my recovery time short. With the help of my surgeon, the company doctor vetoed that idea. When I finally returned to work weeks later, I had a new assignment. Our three departments, which encompassed about 45 programmers, a few support people, our computers, and our wired networks, were slated to move to a new building across the street. I became the technical director for migrating programs and data. I was a month behind schedule before I started.

For those outside our group, it sounded pretty simple, but it was not. Our task was to modify over a thousand programs to run on a different operating system (moving from OS/MVT to OS/MVS) and test them. Many of the original authors (long gone) had used forbidden programming tricks that MVT had tolerated but that MVS would not. I created a conversion list for the dozen or so items. Most of my people had to do it part time while continuing to support their internal customers. There were some other complications as well. After three weeks, my two assistants and I prepared and defended a plan that would take a year to execute.

For some time I had been yearning to get back into systems programming (after nine years in applications programs). Just as the migration plan was getting well under way, a transfer offer was made that excited me. I shared this with my manager, convincing him that one of my assistants could fill whatever vacuum I would leave, and he blessed my move. After nine years in one organization, I moved two blocks down the street within the San Jose IBM plant to the Product Test Laboratory.

As a parting thought to COMATS, in the early 1970s we had occasional visitors from our company's marketing and product development groups, and we soon recognized some of our system's features in trade journal articles about IBM products that carried new names.

The Product Test Laboratory

When I transferred to the IBM San Jose Test Lab in the spring of 1976, I was assigned as Vice-Chief Programmer of a project to create a subsystem named HEX, which we will delve into shortly. The Chief Programmer, Norm, had a total understanding of our application, which I tried to learn quickly. He and I worked very closely together for four years.

Product Test's job was twofold:

1. To determine how well a potential new hardware product performed to its specifications, and
2. To determine how quickly components, especially moving parts, would wear out.

It could be said that a Product Test Lab is the devil's advocate, whose mission it is not so much to praise a product as to find and document its weaknesses. Product Test must have enough independence from the development group to be able to honestly expose whatever flaws a device has, without repercussions.

I, however, never did directly test a machine. I worked on small teams that designed, wrote, and supported software systems which made it easy for test engineers to write and execute simple programs to test hardware. Sometimes I was the team. When one is the system support person for several dozen test engineers, life is interesting.

When a company is developing any new product, it takes a risk with the pending success or failure of that product. The success of most products is dependent not just on their price and performance, but on numerous other parameters, such as timing of announcement and delivery. There is generally a very specific window of time to successfully introduce a new product to the market. So, whenever starting into a testing cycle for a product, there can be no assumptions about its potential success. Most importantly, the product's release depends very much on the testing phase.

HEX, the Hardware EXerciser

With those uncertainties, I spent the next sixteen years providing software to test a variety of hardware products. I first joined three other programmers to create HEX, the Hardware EXerciser. HEX was designed primarily to test ultra-high-speed printers. Development of HEX took us four years full-time (with three more part-time team members) Ultra-high speed meant printing about 2½ pages per second or a 3000-sheet box of paper in 20 minutes. Those printer products paid my salary—took care of my family's food, shelter, schooling, and our other needs—for eight years and made substantial profits for IBM.

In 1980, when HEX made the transition from development to production, I became the singular support person and transferred with it to Tucson, Arizona. I supported two departments of Test Engineers and two departments of Development Engineers (perhaps about thirty) in their use of HEX, in addition to HEX installations at IBM plants in Europe and Japan. I communicated with the overseas folks by email within the IBM worldwide network. If we had to call each other, it was either early in the morning for Europe or late in the afternoon for Japan. I felt good about my contribution to IBM's calculated confidence in marketing a series of successful, profitable high-speed printer products.

HEX would be called a secondary control program. It ran under OS/MVT, but in order to measure a product's performance, HEX (or any other such testing system) had to "steal" I/O interrupts from MVT. It thus became the first-level interrupt handler (FLIH pronounced "flea"). It would process the I/O interrupts for its machines under test and quickly pass each of the other interrupts on to MVT.

HEX also made it easy for development engineers or Product Test engineers to install, for testing, any peripheral device at any unused address without a system generation (sysgen). A sysgen is a time-consuming operation in which the systems programmer recompiles the operating system. This was yet another reason for stealing interrupts. With HEX, I/O addresses were in constant flux, with daily or weekly changes as various machines under test were added to or removed from the system.

The reader might guess (correctly) that the FLIH was one of my responsibilities in the development of HEX. It was relatively easy to do under OS/MVT. Running under OS/MVS created more of a challenge for me. In testing my code where HEX had modified the computer's memory location from which the FLIH gained control, MVS would soon automatically undo my code's work by reestablishing itself as the FLIH. It took me several days to find one of the MVS system experts in IBM who could give me the clues I needed. After searching through microfiche of MVS code, I found the other "flag" in memory that I had to set to mollify MVS.

HEX Testing

For testing additions or changes to HEX, I would run my trial version of HEX under an image of our OS/MVT operating system which, itself, was running under VM. My code had a few "hooks" into MVT. That means I changed a few things in OS normally off limits to applications programmers, such as the FLIH pointer addressed earlier.

Therefore, I needed either a dedicated computer, or a dedicated virtual computer. VM provided the latter for me, sparing IBM a large hardware expense. Whenever I inadvertently damaged OS or did something to crash the system, only my virtual system crashed. Under VM, nobody else was affected.

During the last decade of my career, I worked very closely with Arlen "Pete" Pederson, mostly in Tucson. Pete, in fact, became the technical manager of our test systems group for my last few years there.

By far the most time was spent in finding program bugs, a short time fixing them, and more time testing the fixes. I had a humbling experience (one of many) when I created an I/O queue manager for HEX upon an urgent request by our test engineers. When they were testing two or three printers concurrently on the same data channel, one or more would tend to be "locked out" by another. When an I/O interrupt signaled completion of, say, a write operation, my FLIH would sense a pending request from the same device and start that next I/O to the detriment of other waiting devices.

So, I designed an efficient little I/O queue manager within my FLIH and tested it. The system quickly crashed, under VM, of course. I reinspected my code and retested it with various traces for a week to no avail. Such traces can become voluminous, and will also radically change the timing. In the meantime, my users were getting extremely frustrated with my delay. There was only one person within my reach who had the background to help me, and that was Pete Pederson. He rather quickly "played computer" and discovered that, in a particular code branch, I had restored the general registers from the wrong locations. The fix was in changing the address field of one instruction. We programmers are so familiar with our new code that sometimes we see what we expect to see, not what really is.

Finding a Needle in a Haystack

The following story might help the reader to understand what HEX was all about. Bill, our customer engineer (computer hardware maintenance guy), came into my office in Tucson one day, circa 1982. He wondered if I could help him isolate a hardware glitch somewhere in a bunch of IBM 2260 display terminals. Eight of them were connected to a control unit which, in turn, was connected to a data channel which was connected to the mainframe.

The problem was that at seemingly random intervals the whole group of eight 2260s would crash. The machines might run just fine for only a few hours, or for a week. When they crashed, the work of up to eight test engineers or technicians would suddenly be interrupted. Bill had already swapped out all the functional modules in the control unit, to no avail. It was not practical for him to hook his test instruments to various circuits for days on end, through many thousands of successful transactions, waiting for the axe to fall at some inopportune time for our users.

I told Bill that I could write a simple little Test Case program in a few minutes that would, running under HEX, write any stream of data he desired to any or all of the eight 2260s as fast as they could read. This would compress several days' activity into a few minutes. We made his problem happen not just once, but several times

114

within the hour. Each "hit" helped Bill to isolate the problem further. Within the hour he had isolated it to a circuit in a single 2260 that had, somehow, repeatedly managed to take the whole control unit down when its operator pressed certain keys.

What I want to point out by this little story is that HEX, although it was created to drive certain high-speed printers, could exercise any kind of I/O device at any hardware address with any stream of data or orders that could be put onto a data channel. A small Test Case program would specify what was to happen, and HEX would carry out the operations.

A Successful Failure

In the mid-1980s I spent two years preparing a test system for, and supporting the tests of, a small tape drive before its failures in our tests led to its cancellation. In one way, our test crew felt sad, as if the cost of our test had been a waste of money. On the other hand, we saved IBM a great deal more money, trouble, and reputation, by exposing the problems which doomed the product.

Quality Circles

In the second half of the twentieth century, American businessmen learned from the Japanese about quality circles. IBM was one of the American companies that tried to institute quality circles in the mid-1980s.

In Japan, workers were very loyal to their respective companies, often working through their whole career for one company. Both supervisors and their workers were dedicated, above all else, to helping their company's profitability. In the United States, that bond usually did not exist, especially when a labor union was involved.

In Japan, quality meetings would be held frequently, where all would sit in a circle. Various workers could freely make labor-saving or cost-saving suggestions, and if analysis showed any of them to be valid, management would put those into practice.

In the 1930s, IBM's President, Thomas Watson Sr., started a Suggestion Program, whereby workers could put a suggestion (it had to be outside the worker's normal realm of control) on a form and drop it into a suggestion box. If, after analysis, it was implemented, the worker would receive a percentage of the first year's savings. Over the years, a few of my suggestions were accepted.

The quality circle went a step further, as in Japan. We noted that most of our ideas were rejected because they would impact our schedules negatively. We perceived a tug-of-war between improving quality and making schedule. One often had to suffer for the other to benefit.

Then someone read a quote from an expert who said something like, "Workers naturally take pride in the quality of their work, but are forced by management to take shortcuts." So, at the next quality circle meeting, we pinned our manager down, asking, "If, in doing a task, we find that we must either sacrifice the quality of our work or miss our schedule, which should we choose?"

His answer was, "By all means, never sacrifice quality."

"Then we would maintain quality and slip the schedule?"

Our manager dodged the bullet, saying something like, "Oh, no. Never slip the schedule." At that point we gave up. But, before very many weeks went by, fewer and fewer quality circles were scheduled, until there were no more.

Crystal Balls

My last major task before retiring from IBM was to head a study of requirements for future Product Test systems in Tucson, looking ahead through the decade of the 1990s and into the 21st century. A product revolution was going on within our division (indeed, the world), and we needed some crystal balls, looking into the future for more than just five or ten years.

One day in the second month of the study, during a brainstorming session with one of our testing departments, their manager made a pointed comment, and we suddenly realized that the architecture we had in mind at that time would not satisfy one very important future need.

Nobody, up until then, had made that point. Had it not been for that one lady's remark, we may have continued to create a system that worked perfectly but was of limited use.

Programmers historically have a tendency to design their systems with a severely limited understanding of their customers' needs. The results, too often, are products that perform just right to the wrong specifications.

And just what was that lady's point? Personal computers! Through the 1970s the devices we tested were to be attached to mainframe computers. Minicomputers had crept up slowly during the 1970s decade, but mentalities of IBMers were still either mini or mainframe, depending on where they (we!) worked in IBM (or the industry).

When personal computers (in which I include business-oriented workstations) sprang up in the 1980s, the technology got so far ahead of the culture so fast that we were finally shocked into a realization that the world had changed in ways we had never imagined, and that we had better catch up.

In our small part of the IBM workforce, I think that the test engineers were the ones who first saw the real world, because they were on the firing line. They were the ones who would first recognize and tell us of their needs. We could—if we were lazy—spend a lot of time in our ivory towers, designing systems that "worked perfectly but were of limited use."

Now I will explain and answer the lady manager's question. Simply put, we were no longer to be testing our proposed peripheral devices just on one kind of hardware. Disk drives for micros, for example, were being combined for mainframes into vast arrays of those smaller drives. We had to learn how to test a device on a micro, on a mini, and on a mainframe, because it could or would be installed on any or all of those machines.

Back in 1964 IBM had announced the S/360, a family of computers of different sizes, but of the same architecture. In the 1970s, minis came out of left field with their unique architecture(s), and in the 1980s the PCs had come out of right field with yet another architecture. How could a testing system be written (once) to run on all those systems? The answer became obvious. It had to use a universal language, one common to all the computing "platforms."

With that realization, we reduced our language choices to those that were, or would be, universal among the hardware choices, high-level languages suitable for systems programming. That fact, and its ramifications, caused our systems group to change our methods and even our workstations.

In true IBM fashion, one might say, it took us a year to do the study and specify the general architecture of our future testing software system. Two years after I retired, I ran into Pete and asked him what they were doing.

"We're writing your system," he replied, and that made me feel pretty good.

Part III: Personal Computers

In 1972 my manager at IBM returned from a technical conference and told me something that he had just learned: that in ten years the power of our twin S/360 model 40s would be contained on a desktop. That would be, I tried to imagine, less than a thousandth of the space. I didn't quite believe it at the time. It was beyond my comprehension—but he was right!

I was a programmer of mainframe computers, versus the minicomputers, that had established themselves in the industry during the 1970s. My focus was too narrow to comprehend the energy being spent by professionals and hobbyists alike to create tiny programmable digital devices, affordable to common people.

Integrated circuits (ICs), where many transistors and other components were imbedded on a single chip of silicon, began to replace discrete transistors in the late 1960s. ICs were subjected to various means of miniaturization, leading to the creation of microprocessors. Moore's Law, a prediction of Gordon Moore in 1965, stated that the number of components on a computer chip would double every year. It has been a fairly good rule of thumb for the past four decades.

Part III explores a number of historical personal computer developments along with my own limited experiences.

Chapter 12: The Evolution of PCs

Evolution of Electronic Calculators

It may be a challenge for the younger generations to imagine that we have not had tiny shirt-pocket electronic calculators forever. In the early twentieth century, mechanical calculators—where numbers were keyed in, and a lever pulled to perform an operation—were the best solution up to that era.

In the days when I was a pup (the 1930s and 40s), many offices had large electro-mechanical calculators. A typical one that could multiply and divide was the size of a large desk drawer and weighed enough to discourage many ladies from lifting it. The calculators that could only add and subtract were a quarter that size, but only Paul Bunyan would have had a pocket large enough to carry it on his person.

In the decade of the 1960s, Sharp, WANG, and Hewlett-Packard created and sold transistorized replacements to the old electro-mechanical calculators. They were a sign of progress, but were still big and heavy, and their purchase prices were still in the thousands of dollars.

Integrated circuits had been invented in 1958. About ten years later they began to find their way into the first hand-held calculators produced by Texas Instruments, Hewlett-Packard, and Busicom, a Japanese company. Prices dropped by an order of magnitude into the low to middle hundreds of dollars.

In 1971 the young Intel company, which had been providing chips for Busicom's calculators, marketed the 4004 and 8008, the world's first commercial microprocessor chips. They were created for electronic calculators and terminals, respectively.

The idea that the descendants of those calculator and terminal chips would drive table-top personal computers had not dawned on anybody that I knew in 1971.

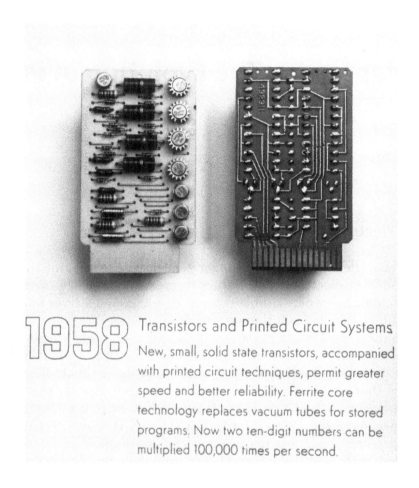

1958 Transistors and Printed Circuit Systems

New, small, solid state transistors, accompanied with printed circuit techniques, permit greater speed and better reliability. Ferrite core technology replaces vacuum tubes for stored programs. Now two ten-digit numbers can be multiplied 100,000 times per second.

Non-Decimal Calculations

Most folks in my generation were quite proficient at arithmetic in the decimal number system; some were not. For either group, a greater challenge was arithmetic in any other number system, such as octal (base 8) or hexadecimal (base 16, often called hex). Our elder generations, including mine, were not taught number system theory in any grade through high school. Number systems, other than decimal, were in the realm of digital computer hardware and software pioneers and few others.

Even those of us who had memorized hexadecimal addition tables had more of a challenge in subtraction. Multiplication and division were tedious, to say the least. When looking inside a raw memory dump of a binary digital computer, we saw octal or hex numbers, depending on the computer architecture, and that was the number system we worked with.

Around 1973 my manager approved the purchase of an electronic calculator that had both decimal and hexadecimal modes. It cost over $400 at that time. We thought it was quite compact—somewhat larger than a big sandwich. Our department's dozen programmers shared it by initialing a sign-out sheet after persuading the current possessor to part with it briefly, by describing our own urgent need for it.

By 1977, the size and price of decimal-hex calculators had decreased to the point where we each had one, and it would fit into a pocket.

Those "little" calculators were the precursors of personal computers. They were dedicated computers, each with a processor chip, random access memory, a keyboard, and a display. The big difference in principle was that its entire program for performing arithmetic operations was permanently locked in read-only memory. I do remember, however, that in the mid-'70s, my son Chuck and I programmed his Commodore calculator to perform a series of calculations. As I recall, one could store about thirty program steps.

The Birth of Personal Computers

Until about 1978, I was one of those who envisioned computers in the workplace only, not in the home. I was not alone. As late as 1977, Ken Olson, president and founder of Digital Equipment Corporation, a company created to manufacture minicomputers, was quoted as saying, "There is no reason anyone would want a computer in their home." How could we have known?

In the early '70s, a plethora of companies, many of them in bedrooms, garages, or other low-cost quarters, took a shot at wealth by marketing microprocessors connected to switches, LEDs, and various other components. Aiming at hobbyists and curious engineers, a few of them made modest profits. Many of them folded.

The Altair

Micro Instrumentation and Telemetry Systems (MITS), a tiny company in Albuquerque, New Mexico known for its various electronic hobby devices and calculator kits, was struggling to remain profitable. When the January 1975 issue of "Popular Electronics" magazine featured a "full-fledged computer," the MITS Altair 8800 as the most powerful microcomputer to date, its sales took off. The Altair 8800 was powered by INTEL's new 8080 microprocessor, the successor to the 8008. The 8008 had 8-bit internal and I/O buses.[1] The 8080 had an 8-bit I/O bus and a 16-bit internal bus, which moved data at about twice the speed of an 8-bit bus.

Although the Altair was far from having the power of the computer in the sky that my manager had predicted, it was an introduction. It was a kit. I don't know about the instructions for building it, but those of at least one of its eventual competitors were such that the skills of an electronic technician or engineer were needed to put it together. Even five years later, when two of my engineer work-associates assembled a couple of computer kits, their strong electronic backgrounds were needed to bridge omissions in the assembly instructions and to isolate and replace defective parts.

Microsoft's First Years

Bill Gates and Paul Allen were among those who saw the Altair article. Few paid much attention to them then, but they saw the need for a BASIC language interpreter on the Altair. Gates and Allen had been "computer nerds" even before their years at Lakeside High School in Seattle, when they had programmed DEC's PDP-10 mini. Drawing on their backgrounds to produce the interpreter, they licensed it to MITS, and Altair sales took off like a rocket. Allen soon became MITS Software Vice President, also remaining in partnership with Gates part-time (and then full-time again in late 1976). Gates' education at Harvard was permanently interrupted. He was too busy supporting Altair BASIC in Albuquerque.

In a short time, Gates and Allen formed a company and named it *Micro-Soft* (later to become *Microsoft*). In 1977 Gates and Allen shipped Microsoft FORTRAN for the 8080, soon followed by BASIC and FORTRAN for the new 8086 microprocessor. MITS became less and less important to Gates as he grew his customer base of MITS competitors and of others to whom his company provided interpreters and compilers for a growing list of languages, as well as computer simulators and other software.

Late in 1978, Microsoft moved from Albuquerque to Bellevue, Washington, near where both Gates and Allen had been raised. At the time, I had heard a rumor that it was because Microsoft couldn't get a loan in Albuquerque, and Bill's attorney

---

1   In an 8-bit bus, instructions and data are transferred, 8 bits at a time, each on one of 8 parallel conductors (called a bus).

dad had arranged one in Seattle if they would move there. That, I learned much later, was not true! Microsoft was essentially debt-free with a six-figure savings account by then and supposedly didn't need a loan.

When Microsoft generated a new product, it would include significant new capabilities, but save some for version 2. Again, version 2 would include some additional marketable features, but save some for version 3, and so on. Many companies follow that practice, making incremental money from each new version.

Commodore's Pet and other offerings

The creation of the Altair launched a large number of competitors, such as IMSAI, whose offerings were more reliable, more capable, or more economical.

In 1976–77, Commodore, famous for their calculators, produced a preassembled out-of-the-box computer based on MOS Technology's 6502 chip. It was named the Commodore PET, which stood for *Personal Electronic Transactor*. It was the first computer to have Microsoft BASIC permanently embedded in read-only memory (ROM), much to the delight of BASIC users, who no longer had to load BASIC from other media.

In the early 1970s, Texas Instruments was also developing a computer, code-named SP-70, using TI's own chip, and Microsoft BASIC. Radio Shack also joined the fray, introducing its TRS-80 with a stripped-down BASIC. Later, they too would invest in the use of Microsoft BASIC in order to be competitive.

Growing an Apple

In 1976 Stephen G. Wozniak created a computer based on MOS Technology's inexpensive 6502 chip, which could outperform the Altair and sell for a fraction of its price. Woz had a penchant for simple, yet powerful, designs. He was a technocrat, a self-made engineer, a creator. He had no interest in spending his time trying to market it beyond demonstrating it to peers at the Homebrew Computer Club in Palo Alto, California. His friend, Steven P. Jobs, filled that vacuum. Several manufacturing and marketing efforts failed before Jobs finally found a venture capitalist to fund it.

They called their company *Apple*,[2] and the computer *Apple I*. With their cash transfusion, Apple could move out of Job's parents' garage and into its own space.

2　Jobs had picked apples in the Northwest. The company was so named, reportedly, because of the attributes of apples: resistant to damage, nutritional, and well-packaged—the "perfect fruit."

Countering the lack of capability or appeal the Apple I had for business use (it had only 4K of high-speed memory), it was a great hit with hobbyists, and sales were brisk.

In 1977, Apple introduced the Apple II Personal Computer. Sales were difficult with Woz's rather primitive Integer BASIC (later replaced with an enhanced version of Microsoft's 6502 BASIC for a price paid to Microsoft).

During the same period, Dan Bricklin and Bob Frankston had written a program that would let a user create a chart of numbers and do arithmetic on them. They first called it Calculedger: a ledger program that could do calculations.

Calculedger was renamed the *Visible Calculator* and shortened to *VisiCalc*, the first computerized spreadsheet program, and installed on the Apple II. VisiCalc is said to have "sold" 200,000 Apple IIs in the next two years.

How much would I have spent for a program like that (and a machine to run it on)? For years, in order to minimize the emergencies caused by sudden surprising shortages in my growing family's funds, I had projected our income and expenses for the next few pay periods *by hand* on such a chart. Here was a program that would automate the calculations. Had VisiCalc been available to me back in the mid-1970s, I would have had only to add a little bit of new data each month instead of creating holes in the paper with my erasures (and periodically rewriting the chart).

Vital Early Software

VisiCalc became the forerunner of a dozen or more such programs whose creators aspired to wealth. Some of them had a relatively short life. One exception was VisiCalc's earliest competitor, announced by a company called Lotus. The product was named Lotus 1-2-3. Over the next decade, competing spreadsheets would repeatedly leapfrog each other in sophistication, and a few new players with sufficient financial backing would join the fray. One of these was Microsoft, who announced the first very flaky version of Excel in 1985. It finally shipped in October 1987, two years late. (Bill's early philosophy was to announce first, fix later.) Another spreadsheet creator was Microsoft's nemesis in the languages arena: Borland International, with their Quattro Pro.

Hardware, per se, did not sell itself well, except to hobbyists. Aside from game software, hardware marketers needed applications software that would solve business problems for potential customers. One such early application was a product initially called *Electronic Paper* that could format documents for printing.

Electronic Paper made its commercial debut under the name *Multiplan* and was a resounding success. Recognizing its potential, Bill Gates of Microsoft and Steve Jobs of Apple met with its developers in mid-1981 to license Multiplan. Jobs had in mind that Microsoft would simply adapt it for the Apple II. While doing that, Gates was ever looking for leveraging opportunities. Multiplan competitors, such as *Word-Star,* sprung up quickly. The IBM PC had its rudimentary *EasyWriter.*

Other Hardware

In 1978 Dennis Glayes developed the modem. The name is a contraction of *modulator-demodulator.* By modulating the digital signals from a computer onto high frequency waves, called a *carrier,* data could be sent from a computer over an ordinary phone line. At the receiving end the signal would be demodulated, separating the data from the carrier, and stored in the processor's memory for further use. The modem provided another means for computers to share information.

There were numerous other computers being built by various companies, each of whom intended to get a share of what they perceived to be a lucrative market. Several of those who had avoided buying Bill Gates' software products initially would do so later. Microsoft BASIC had become a de-facto standard and was demanded by potential buyers. That gave Gates the opportunity to bundle some of his other language products for an additional fee! Microsoft had a knack for cultivating and winning its competitors' customers, leveraging any one software product on its other software and a few hardware products. With about a dozen employees, it was cranking out software at a furious pace and collecting the rewards.

CP/M

In the early 1970s, at least a few pioneers had begun to realize that a rudimentary operating system would be needed to support the evolving capabilities of microcomputers.

One of these was Gary Kildall of Digital Research in California. Starting with a subset of Digital Equipment Corporation's TOPS-10 (for PDP-10 minicomputers), he created CP/M (Control Program for Microcomputers), a basic operating system that could be crammed into the very limited memory of a microcomputer.

CP/M became very popular, albeit with a large number of variations introduced either by changing external equipment interfaces, squeezing part of it into less space, or adding features. Gates had a wide vision of future sales, and CP/M was part of that vision. CP/M played a role in the creation of DOS.

The File Allocation Table

External storage media on micros were tending to evolve from the likes of cassette tapes to *diskettes*, better known as "floppy" disks. Records were written and read on tape in serial fashion. When the end of tape was reached, it was full, simple as that. No space allocation algorithm was needed. Disks, of course, could also have been designed to operate only sequentially, but that would have wasted their capabilities as random access devices.

I remember first seeing the 8-inch-diameter floppy disks at IBM, circa 1970. Like its 5¼-inch successor, it consisted of a flexible round disk with a magnetic coating and a metal hub, all encased in a jacket with access holes through which magnetic heads could read or write.

The 8-inch disks that I saw were hidden inside the covers of control units for the hard-disk storage devices that IBM was then manufacturing (roughly 3 feet square and 6 feet tall) for mainframe computers. The floppy disk contained microcode (programs written by hardware engineers) for a dedicated processor in the control unit that enabled it to manage a long row of disk drives in their cabinets.

The 8-inch drive tended to be too big and cumbersome for a microcomputer. The advent of a 5¼-inch disk changed all that. The costs of drives and diskettes decreased dramatically with time and with volume shipped.

Disk drives' great benefit was random access to programs and data, but that created a new problem, that of efficiently recording data and managing the allocation of space and the sequence of data on disk. A resourceful programmer named Marc McDonald solved the problem for the NCR 8200 by creating a compact table to reside in high-speed memory. He named it the *file allocation table*, or FAT, and it eventually became standard on many microcomputers.

Birth of the IBM PC

While working for IBM in the 1980-81 timeframe, I was told through our rumor mill that John Opel, IBM's Chairman of the Board, had noted the microcomputer revenues of Apple, Radio Shack, Commodore, and other PC makers and asked what the company's plans were regarding PCs. As the rumor went, there were none, and

Opel ordered the company into action. Like most rumors, most of it was fiction!

IBM, unknown to most of us immersed in its other endeavors, had been making significant investments in microcomputer projects (that were not particularly user-friendly) over the past two years or more.

Another story tells us that, at a meeting of the Corporate Management Committee in July 1980, Bill Lowe, the Boca Raton (Florida) Lab Director, heard Opel remark about his dissatisfaction with that project. Lowe offhandedly said he could do it in a year from start to finish. However that part of the story really went, Lowe was challenged by Opel to make a formal proposal in a month.

IBM had a long-established "mainframe mentality." An influential segment of company management, most of whom were associated with mainframes, pooh-poohed the idea of micros ever having an influence in the business market. After all, were they not just hobby toys? Others feared that successes in microcomputers would devastate the mainframe segment of the business, IBM's "bread and butter." Even IBM's established "small systems" (minicomputers) had a constant uphill fight at the corporate level.

Major IBM products typically had a four- or five-year development cycle, justified on very large and complex systems. The company was just not accustomed to the rapid pace required for the fast-changing microcomputer market. Bill Lowe's group had to break through that mentality.

A Wild Duck Task Force

Back in Boca Raton, Lowe set up a task force of a dozen trusted employees to re-explore the market, determine feasibility, and establish specifications for a system that could be assembled from components that already existed. Most of the task force consisted of "wild ducks."

An Acorn Grows

At the meeting in August, Lowe demonstrated some moving images on a tiny computer, made a convincing presentation, and got the go-ahead from the CMC. The project was code-named *Chess*, and the product, *Acorn*. A hectic schedule of hardware integration and software development began. Lowe assigned Don Estridge to head the effort. Lowe had to get back to his real job—managing the entire Boca Raton plant. Estridge was another *wild duck* with a reputation of getting things done, well-known to Lowe, and a perfect fit for the task at hand. He was no stranger to micro-computers. He owned an Apple II and spent many hours at home exploring what he could do on it.

Because of the tight schedule and the need to use proven components, Acorn could not be a state-of-the-art system. One slight departure from that strategy was to use a much faster processor than the 2MHz Intel 8080. Two were available:

- The Intel 8086, with 16-bit internal and external buses, introduced in 1978 as successor to the 8080 and 8085, at a speed of 4.77 MHz.
- The Intel 8088, with a 16-bit internal bus and 8-bit external bus was a stripped down version of the 8086, introduced later in 1978.

The 8088 processor was chosen over the 8086 because most available accessories and peripheral devices were still 8-bit, and it cost less.

Another significant decision was made to leave extra space between components inside the case to avoid potential cooling problems, especially in hostile environments. An extension of this idea was to allocate space and circuitry for so-called *expansion slots*, by which owners could install a variety of add-on circuit boards for extra memory, a modem, connections to a variety of external devices, a clock-calendar, and numerous other functions.

The PC could have one or two 5¼-inch diskette drives. At the time, floppy disks were single-sided and could hold 160K characters. Later, they would boost 160K to 180K. Still later, the floppy would become double-sided, for a total of 360K. It would, in a few years, be replaced by a 5¼-inch diskette that could contain a megabyte. A smaller 3½-inch diskette that held 1.4 MB made the 1 MB floppy obsolete before its use became widespread.

Not the least of the problems was the advertising campaign. They had to do "one better" than the highly successful Apple ads. After many false starts, the (Charley Chaplin) tramp figure, with his red rose, finally emerged as central to the campaign. The tramp succeeded in transforming the image of a cold, stodgy IBM into a company with a face.

By using proven components, many matters of parts quality and quantity had been resolved, but development of certain software components was one of the biggest, if not *the* biggest, cliffhanger.

DOS

Part of the challenge was in putting an operating system and applications software together quickly. Microsoft, still a small company with a few dozen programmers, owned FORTRAN, COBOL, BASIC, and Pascal language processors which were widely used and which could be adapted for the 8088 and the operating system. It was a challenging but not a formidable task. It was a matter of developing contractual arrangements, finding or developing enough trained staff, and going to work.

At one of their meetings with Microsoft, an IBMer mentioned the need for an operating system. It would be necessary to acquire and certify an operating system quickly, so as to supply it to vendors of applications software for testing their programs.

Microsoft recommended CP/M and arranged a meeting between themselves, IBM, and Digital Research (CP/M's owner). In the meeting DR would not agree to IBM's nondisclosure agreement (and most likely—from hindsight—would not have produced an 8088 version of CP/M in time anyhow). Gates told IBM that he may just know someone else who could supply an operating system.

Gates and Allen knew Tim Paterson and Rod Brock of Seattle Computer Products, which had developed an operating system for the 8086 based largely on CP/M commands. Paterson had departed from strictly cloning CP/M, electing to use Marc McDonald's File Allocation Table (FAT) invention. He also improved command syntax and made other changes. They variously named their system QDOS (Quick and Dirty Operating System) and SCP-DOS (Seattle Computer Products Disk Operating System).

Because of his experience with royalties paid to MITS in the early days, Gates was determined to avoid paying royalties for each copy of the operating system. He talked to SCP and licensed it at a fixed $50,000 for an "unnamed manufacturer's" computer, and others. Gates then demonstrated and relicensed it to IBM, in a non-exclusive contract, with a royalty to be paid to Microsoft for each copy.

In their early business relationship, Microsoft was alternately a source of concern and a hero to IBM's PC developers. They were already behind schedule when they signed the contract and were struggling to make up time. On the other hand, Gates and Allen had contacts throughout the microcomputer world and were quite possibly the only ones who could reach out to certain players and products in the extremely short time frame necessary.

IBM would have much preferred to write its own software if it thought it could have done so in time. IBM fully intended, from the time they signed the contract, to take over DOS at some point in time. Gates and Allen knew that and intended to milk the profits as hard and as long as they could.

Three years later (1984), Microsoft had also licensed its MS-DOS to about two hundred other personal computer makers, establishing itself as the source of *the* standard operating system for personal computers, and feeding an enormous growth in the market for personal computers.

From Acorn to Oak Tree

The IBM Personal Computer was announced on schedule on August 12, 1981 with well over a thousand units already in Sears Business Centers and Computerland retail stores, ready to sell. This was an amazing record in a company with a four-year product cycle and with no experience in outside retail distribution.

When IBM announced its Personal Computer, it gave credence to the PC business. Whereas computers had once been thought to be for engineers and hobbyists, now PCs were for anyone. Many *"anyones"* soon learned, through their own experiences, how steep the learning curve was.

The PC had 16K of random-access memory (RAM) and a 160K 5¼-inch diskette drive for $1,595. IBM had made sure that some basic programs were available:

- Microsoft BASIC, burned into ROM
- VisiCalc (matching the Apple II)
- EasyWriter, a basic word processor
- Peachtree business programs.

These applications would match, more or less, what the competition had. What it had that major competitors did not, were two well-guarded secrets:

- Expansion slots. Vendors would create hundreds of different plug-in card applications, starting an entirely new sub-industry. Expansion card developers correctly surmised that there was little risk in creating PC cards.
- DOS was an "open" system, which meant anyone who could learn the BASIC programming language (or any other for which a PC assembler, compiler or interpreter was available) and create a program, install it, and run it on DOS, could sell it without anyone else's help or permission.

This was in vivid contrast to the closed hardware architecture in IBM's most significant competitor's offering at that time, the Apple II.

IBM PC, circa 1981

Response from the American marketplace (and, later, overseas) was beyond anybody's imagination. Demand very soon exceeded manufacturing capacity. Production was quickly tripled and quadrupled. It was not just a matter of IBM's capacity, but very much a matter of parts suppliers' ability to ramp up their deliveries.

Over 13,000 PCs were sold in those first four months at the end of 1981. Sales were just getting started. In 1982 the nation woke up to the point that "Time Magazine's" staff departed from their traditional "Man of the Year" recognition to name the personal computer as its "Machine of the Year for 1982" in the 1983 opening issue.

Programming History Repeated

There came a flood of new programs. Many of them were the first programs ever written by their respective authors and were riddled with bugs that caused them to malfunction, sometimes catastrophically. Bugs were by no means new in the computer industry. Unintentional errors in programs were as old as the industry itself. What was new was a self-taught generation of brand-new programmers with nobody to teach them techniques and pitfalls. Slowly, it improved as the new programmers learned proven programming practices the hard way and discovered that rigorous testing is necessary. In the meantime, thousands of buyers of error-prone software were exposed to sometimes-disastrous consequences. For the most part, they patiently used *workarounds* until fixes could be installed or programs replaced.

I had seen this happen before. *Micro-coded devices* had popped up at IBM starting in the 1960s. Examples were control units for disk drives, printers, and other peripheral devices that had their own pre-programmed brains, invisible to the customer.

IBM had dedicated cadres of experienced programmers who wrote operating systems or program products to be used by its customers. We also had programming groups who wrote code for the internal needs of their respective parts of the company. When control units for peripheral devices containing their own little processors were first created, the development engineers, lacking access to professional programming groups took on the task of micro-programming those devices without formal programmer training. As a result, they learned about good and bad programming practices the hard way! I had witnessed that first-hand from my years in the Product Test Lab, so when I saw the same things happen in the PC business, it was *deja vu*.

Computer Clocks

The IBM 709x series did not have a real-time clock, nor did its standard operating systems have a system clock.

As our predecessors had done before us, we early-1960s programmers learned about Gregorian and Julian calendars and about converting dates from one to the other. As the years passed, and as new operating systems came along, they began including utilities to perform date calculations, and real-time clocks began showing up in mainframe computers. I suppose the real solution awaited the advent of the tiny long-life battery, which is needed to power the real-time clock when commercial power is off.

Those who had personal computers before the mid-1980s perhaps remember that the early IBM PCs and their clones had no electronic clock.

Unless you bought a special card containing what is called a *real-time clock*, removed the cover from the computer, and installed the electronic clock card and its software, your PC could not remember the date, much less advance it, when the computer was turned off. You would be prompted for the date and time whenever you "IPLed" (Initial Program Load) or "booted up" in the language of PC aficionados.

One way or the other, DOS would load its *system clock* (which is really not a clock but simply a counter) with an integer value representing the number of time units elapsed since January 1, 1980. From the system clock, DOS's utilities performed the time and date functions that were most needed by users. When the battery died, you could tell by the way dates reverted to 1-1-1980.

PC Clubs

Many of the folks who bought microcomputers in the late 1970s and early '80s soon discovered that they were on a steep learning curve concerning their newly-acquired—or proposed—hardware and software. For example, where would a neophyte acquire the courage and the skill to install a clock/calendar card and its software? It took guts for most people to remove the cover from their brand new strange machine, and much more to plug in a card.

To answer the need, many computer clubs (users groups) were formed throughout the world. One member might be proficient with pluggable memory modules, another with monitors, other hardware, or various software offerings. A novice found membership in such a group extremely attractive, if not essential.

A year before I bought my first PC, I joined the newly-formed Tucson IBM Employees' PC Club to learn as much as possible. The Association of Personal Computer User Groups (APCUG) was created to help share the efforts of all the PC Clubs. In the next few years, as manufacturers and suppliers improved support of their customers, many PC clubs died off, but the stronger ones survived, along with the APCUG. These many years later, I still belong to the PC club I joined, even though I'm now seven hundred miles distant. I still clip articles concerning new products and technology advances from the newsletters.

IBM PC Follow-Ons (1980s)

Apple Computer's Steve Jobs welcomed the IBM PC when it made its advent in August 1981, because it established credibility for the personal computer industry. It helped sell Apple IIs initially. He soon changed his mind. When the IBM PC's phenomenal sales eroded Apple's market share, Jobs "declared war" on IBM. It reached its peak with Apple's introduction of Macintosh. Later, as the result of a 1984 survey, Apple realized that its potential customers wanted compatibility between the two companies' products. Apple surprised the industry with a large banner proclaiming: "APPLE DECLARES DETENTE WITH IBM" at its 1985 annual meeting.

I did not buy one of the earliest PCs. I experimented with one at work. I remember wondering which way to turn the floppy disk to insert it. With over twenty years of programming experience behind me at that point, I decided to delay my purchase until a model with a hard disk came out.

In February 1982, six months after the original PC announcement, and while Entry Systems was struggling to increase PC production, their development of three future products was funded by the Corporate Management Committee. They were the PC/XT, the PCjr, and the PC/AT. Each is addressed below.

All but one of the following seven IBM PCs were purchased by members of my immediate family, thanks in part to IBM's employee-family discounts.

IBM PC/XT

The model I had waited for, the PC/XT, was announced (on time) in March 1983. After Lorraine and I explored the Employee Sales terms and our home budget for a week, I ordered one. As a tradeoff for our employee discount, we were put into a quota queue. Orders for the XT far exceeded expectations, so my discounted machine did not come for six months. For it and a 9-pin dot matrix printer, our discounted price was well over $4000.

For a little over $4000, we got a computer with an 8088 processor, a color display, 256K of main memory (128K was standard), a 5¼-inch diskette drive, and a 10MB hard disk. I soon added a clock-calendar card and enough memory to give us

640K total. We acquired a spreadsheet program named PC-CALC and a rudimentary database program named PC-File. I got a free family budget program named PF (Personal Finance), and later PF2, from the IBM network, thanks to its author, an IBMer who wrote it with the original intent of selling it, later deciding to offer it for free.

Our older son, Chuck, who had done time-sharing at his high school back in the early 1970s, was a recently-discharged computer tech from the U.S. Navy submarine service. Chuck was back in our roost to attend the University of Arizona. He became our systems programmer and database administrator. My wife Lorraine, who was trying to keep track of Boy Scout leader training records, began tracking the training of leaders—eventually over 2000 of them—on our PC/XT for the local BSA Council. We generated our first Christmas letter that year, 1983, on the XT.

IBM bought me a 1200-baud modem (pretty fast compared to the 300-baud modems that were generally in use at the time). I was soon able to use a 3270-emulator program to access that great computer in the sky (mainframe) at the IBM plant, 15 miles distant, saving me from a few unplanned late-night emergency support trips to work.

IBM and Sears jointly created Prodigy, an early online support program. One could send and receive email, and access commercial vendors via Prodigy. I got a very cheap year on its net during Prodigy's beta-test. IBM sold its interest somewhat later. After a year on Prodigy (1985), I switched to America Online. Finally, in the early '90s, such networks were allowed to connect to the Internet.

One time an electrical spike caused a hard disk error. The PC began to crash every time we tried to do a particular thing. Chuck and I used our combined brains, a set of system utilities, and a whole Saturday to narrow the problem down to one single binary bit on the hard disk. After proving to ourselves (several times) that we really had the culprit, we got up the courage to flip that bit. It worked! We did that rather than restore from a non-current backup. We did our backups in those days to a continuum of two or three dozen floppy disks. Backups were awkward, lacking high-volume external storage (unless one had a tape drive).

Our XT was worked pretty hard for about seven years. We often had to schedule, informally at least, our time on it. In 1989 the 10MB hard drive crashed. During the previous six years, disk drive technology had evolved to pack twice as much data in half the space. We bought a 20MB replacement drive that was nicknamed a *half-high*. In the remaining space, we installed a 3½-inch diskette drive. I was looking forward to a new computer in a year or so, and wanted to graduate from 5¼-inch diskettes to 3½-inch disks. With both sizes installed in the XT, we eventually migrated all our data to the 3½-inch disks.

When we finally bought a PS/2 in December 1990, the XT went to our daughter Natalie and her husband, Mark. They used it to help run his landscape business for a couple years.

IBM PC Junior

Because of the outstanding successes of the PC and the PC/XT, several dozen media weeklies and monthlies hyped the Junior excessively, especially prior to its announcement on November 1, 1983, (about the time my family's XT was delivered). The PCjr was announced, six months late, with first customer shipments after the holidays because of production problems. The ill-fated PCjr, code-named *Peanut*, had been touted as a "home computer" rather than a "home business computer."

Mary (another of our daughters, 700 miles distant) wanted a PCjr, so I arranged for her to buy it through an employee family sales arrangement.

The basic PCjr sold for $699. It used an Intel 8088 microprocessor (like its two predecessors), had 64K of permanent ROM, 64K of main memory, a 62-key keyboard and two ROM plug-in slots. Mary's also had a 5¼-inch 360K floppy drive and an additional 64K of main memory.

The Junior was not totally compatible with the PC and the XT, partly due to its limited main memory. It was said to be upgradeable to functionally match the PC and the XT. At one of the PC Club meetings I attended, there was displayed (by its proud owner) a PCjr that had been so expanded by an internal-external combination. It was surrounded by a maze of signal wires and power cables for the external add-ons that were plugged into power strips (plural).

The keyboard could work in cordless mode, using an infra-red beam. Its keys looked like Chiclet candies, so it was dubbed the *chiclet keyboard* by the industry. Mary played some games on it, wrote some letters, and didn't do much more.

Customer and media reactions to the chiclet keys were so negative that IBM offered to replace the keyboard for free, if one elected to do so. Mary generally plugged her keyboard into the computer to save battery power. At some point in time, her dog chewed on the connecting cord, and after that, she went with battery power.

The PCjr was "taken out of production" in 1985. In actuality, production ended in mid-1984, with enough inventory (350,000 units) to last another 18 months.

I feel the need to make a point about IBM's bureaucracy on one hand and wild ducks on the other hand. Much of the so-called bureaucracy, not only in IBM but in many mature companies, is really (largely) a system of checks and balances. There was a degree of luck involved with the original PC project. In the interest of saving time, many shortcuts were taken, bypassing checks and balances. The PC marketing group vastly underestimated the demand for their product. The PCjr's market projectors had a major problem in not fully understanding their market, making far too many PCjrs.

You might note as you read on, that the absence of checks and balances added great risk of making bad projections. New fast-growing companies are particularly prone to such problems. Sales projections for Apple's first several computers were alternately vastly overestimated or greatly underestimated.

The IBM Portable PC

In February 1984 the Portable PC was announced. Our son-in-law Frank, (husband of yet another daughter, Nancy), wanted one for his cabinet shop, so we arranged another family-of-employee sale for him.

The Portable PC was resistant to dirty environments. It had a case about the size of the PC or XT, but a 5-inch orange monitor was built into the case. It also had two 5¼-inch floppy drives. Frank used it in his cabinet shop for well over a decade.

In 1993, one of the diskette drives failed. We stripped the computer down to clean it and lubricate the sliders for the access mechanisms on both diskette drives. Frank used it another five years. I'd bet it would still run all these years later if it were to be resurrected out of computer heaven.

About 1998 we replaced our four-year-old Acer laptop with a new one and gave Frank the old laptop. It was his introduction to Windows (version 3.1). He quickly moved his DOS applications from the Portable to Windows, and never looked back.

Frank probably never knew that the Portable was declared a failure and taken off the market within a year and a half of its introduction, mostly due to lack of demand for large, bulky portables.

IBM PC/AT

Intel had developed the 80286 microprocessor chip, dubbed the 286. It ran about three times the speed of the 8088, which was used in all the PCs above. In August, 1984, IBM announced the PC/AT, based on the 286. It came with 3MB of main memory, breaking the 640K barrier imposed by the old 8088, and it had a 20MB hard drive.

139

Initial demand seemed to exceed the supply. Nobody in my family was in the market for a $4000 computer at this time, so we passed by the PC/AT.

The AT might have been a success except for a vendor's part that caused data on hard disks to disappear. Owners complained loudly that they had lost various amounts of data. The buck was passed between the vendors of (1) the disk drive, (2) the controller, and (3) the operating system, with IBM in the middle until the problem was found in a chip (supplied by yet another company) in the controller. By the time the problem was finally resolved, the total delay of nine months in further deliveries dampened the desires of the market.

IBM PC Convertible

In April 1986 IBM announced the PC Convertible, a laptop PC with the Intel 80088 microprocessor, LCD screen, and two 3½-inch floppy disk drives. For several reasons, the Convertible was not popular in the marketplace, but we gave one to our son Chuck upon his graduation from the University of Arizona that June, because we thought he would be moving out of our house, away from our XT.

Chuck used the Convertible for several years and did not move out for seven plus years. Yes, our eldest, who had left the nest first (for the Navy) and returned, was the last of seven siblings to finally leave, just before we sold the house and moved into our motorhome.

IBM Personal System/2

In April of 1987 IBM announced four models of the PS/2. Model 30 was based on the 16-bit 8086 processor, limited to 640K of memory. Models 50 and 60 used Intel's 80286 processors and broke the 640K memory limit of the 8088 and 8086 with 1MB memory, expandable. Model 80 used the 80386 processor, with more power than many minicomputers. By the time we bought a PS/2 at the end of 1990, there were also models 25, 55 SX and 65 SX.

We bought the 55 SX with Windows 3.0 on top of DOS 4.0, 2MB memory, 30MB hard disk, and a 3½-inch diskette drive. With an $800 IBM 4019 laser printer (now Lexmark) included, the employee cost after rebates was about $3500. In the next two years, prices decreased significantly. The printer was our primary printer for 20 years, exhausting numerous new or rebuilt toner cartridges, several bottles of toner, and dozens of cases of paper. Its print quality remained exemplary throughout.

In May 1992 we bought a PS/2 L40SX, which was a laptop computer to supplement the 55 SX for our business, for about $1500. It had an 80386 processor that ran at 20MHz (twice the speed of a 286), a 10-inch monochrome VGA LCD screen, a 60MB hard drive, 2MB memory, built-in modem, and a diskette drive.

IBM Personal System/1

In June 1990 IBM introduced the PS/1 computer for the home, in an attempt to remedy the PCjr image. How was it that the PS/1 was announced three years after the PS/2? I do not know.

The PS/1 was touted as "A serious machine that's simple to use." Taking a cue from Apple, a family would "simply take it out of the box, plug it in, and turn it on with the touch of a button." It used the 80286 processor and came with Windows 3.0 and Microsoft Works installed.

Our daughter Mary and her husband Scott bought a PS/1 with our IBM Employee/Family Sales discount for $1499 (list $1999). It replaced her limited and aging PCjr, which she donated to her Aunt Pat. Their PS/1 had a VGA color monitor, 1MB RAM, a 30MB hard disk, a 3½-inch (1.44MB) diskette drive, and a 2400-bps modem (state of the art at that time).

Chapter 13: Graphical User Interfaces

The *Networks* section of Part II referred to a Pentagon-funded computer research laboratory, known as the Advanced Research Projects Agency (ARPA). During a federal budget crunch (circa 1970) funds for non-military projects were curtailed and some of ARPA's best brains left the agency.

Xerox was interested in such research also, and several of the ex-ARPA researchers went to work for Xerox at its new state-of-the-art computing center, the Palo Alto Research Center in California, or PARC. Many ideas and concepts from ARPA migrated to PARC.

One of the projects carried over to PARC was the idea of graphics on a cathode-ray tube attached to a computer. The few CRT computer terminals that existed outside of PARC could form characters on the screen, typically a dozen lines of 40 characters each, but the graphics idea required a different technology, both in hardware and software.

To do graphics, the screen was divided into a dense pattern—rows of dots called *Picture Elements* (*PELs* then, more commonly known now as *Pixels*), as on a television screen. By design, they were so close together that our eyes would not see the individual dots, but rather the picture they formed. There might be, for example, 480 rows of 640 PELs each, lit selectively by an electron beam scanning the PEL locations. A drawing to be displayed would be converted to a digital form that would turn the beam on and off in just the right sequence to create an image of that drawing on the screen.

In 1963 at the Stanford Research Center in Palo Alto—a short distance from PARC—an engineer named Doug Engelbart had proposed a device for pointing to objects on a computer screen that, because of its appearance, became known as a mouse.

Most people laughed at the idea then but, in the 1970s, it took root at PARC in one of the earliest personal computers, called the Alto.

Around 1979 Apple's Steve Jobs was invited to tour PARC, was captivated by the idea of graphics on the screen, and proceeded to develop graphical user interfaces (GUIs) in his own lab.

A year or two later, in the midst of Apple's frequent dealings with Microsoft, Jobs showed Gates a demonstration of graphics in Apple's lab. Back at Microsoft, Paul Allen was briefed by Gates. They both perceived the advantage that a GUI would give to Apple's Computers over other personal computers.

Apple contracted with Microsoft to develop GUI software for Apple's *Lisa* computer project, announced very prematurely in January 1983. While a cadre of Microsoft programmers worked on the Apple contract, Gates had much wider visions. Microsoft's contract with Apple contained a noncompete clause for one year, until New Year's 1984. By that time, Apple's Lisa had already failed as a competitive product. The GUI would have to wait for the Macintosh, "introduced" in January of 1984 but still months from release.

In the meantime, young Bill tried to convince IBM, which was already in its fourth decade of building and selling computers, of the need for a GUI on future PCs, with the intent of bidding a contract to develop the scheme. IBM saw the need for a new and more powerful interface manager but initially nixed the graphics idea for the next year or so. Perhaps the Apple Macintosh's GUI, developed by Microsoft, changed some minds.

IBM had intended from the beginning to eventually take over the development of DOS, to bring it in-house as was their standard practice. Their new PC/AT, with the much more powerful Intel 80286 processor, was in development and would be announced in late summer 1984. In 1983 they were developing new system software, with the internal name "Topview." It did not have a graphical interface. The intent was that Microsoft would soon be on its own (although the final parting would not occur for another seven years). Topview was finally released in early 1985.

Bill Gates still had a working relationship with IBM's PC developers, and so Microsoft continued to help IBM, in this case with DOS and Topview. IBM had been pressuring Microsoft to turn over the source code for DOS, and that finally happened in the summer of 1985. That would resolve DOS development conflicts between the companies, allowing IBM to market "PC-DOS," and Microsoft "MS-DOS." Although they seemed to be much the same to the casual user, Microsoft was developing MS-DOS to support the features it needed for its GUI.

Microsoft went on to develop IBM's OS/2 for them, finally replacing Topview with a graphical interface. When our daughter Mary replaced her PCjr with a PS/1, she ordered it with OS/2 as the primary operating system, and Windows 3.0 (see below) running under OS/2. Which of those two systems would win the "war of the operating systems" would not be resolved for another five years.

Windows

Gates believed that the 80286 processor had the power and the features needed to support a GUI. When he could not develop it with IBM's money, he decided to do it inhouse with Microsoft's own dollars. It would run on top of DOS. Programmers call such systems *secondary control programs*, because they use the tools and interfaces of the primary control program (DOS, in this case) and add new features on top. This new system would be called "Windows."

The history of software development is full of project overruns, both in time and money. Programmers most often cannot base an estimate on past experiences, because most of our software creations are unlike any program we've created previously. Otherwise we could simply copy and/or modify it, in which case we are still usually late. Windows was no exception. The farther the team got into its development, the more unanticipated work they discovered. Initially promised for April 1984, a beta test version was finally released in February 1985. It was replete with bugs and had few applications programs to go with it.

In concept, Windows was a hit, but its problems and lack of application programs held sales back. Companies that wrote PC application software were short on time and programmers. They tended to develop for the most popular (therefore, profitable) interface which, at the time, was DOS. Application software developers watched Windows with caution, waiting to see if it would become a major player.

Many early problems were resolved with Windows 2.0 in 1987, and sales of Windows improved. The number of applications increased slowly through the late '80s, as Windows struggled to achieve the critical mass it needed. In May 1990, Windows 3.0 was released. Significantly more dependable than previous versions, it was the turning point for software. Suddenly, it seemed, everyone wanted to adapt their software for Windows. Microsoft's 1990 sales topped $1 billion. The appearance of Version 3.1 early in 1992 fixed Version 3.0's most critical remaining bugs. Microsoft's Windows had finally won the war of the operating systems. We didn't hear so much about OS/2 (or DOS) after that.

Epilogue: A Whole New World

I believe that the nature of the computer industry changed much more in the 1980s and 1990s than in its entire prior history. Those years saw not only a phenomenal growth, but a realignment of the industry to personal computers that none of the experts had predicted. The first big change, as I see it, was the phenomenal growth of the market for personal computers. There were said to be:

10,000 computers in the world in 1960
100,000 computers in the world in 1970
100,000,000 computers in the world in 1990
Over a billion computers in the world in 2010

There were no home computers on the 1960 and 1970 lines. By 1990 the vast majority, personal computers, were not just home computers, but microcomputers serving as personal work stations in industry. Now the computer you use most of the time just might be the smart phone in your pocket, more powerful than a room full of machines and it makes phone calls too.

I wish to pay due respect to countless individuals, whether mentioned or not in this book, but in my mind, no two people had more influence in creating the phenomenon I just described than Bill Gates and Steve Jobs.

Some things come around, full circle. Bill Gates was introduced to graphical user interfaces by Steve Jobs and was paid to learn the basics about GUIs through his first GUI contract with Apple (for the Lisa computer). His development of GUIs, outside of his contract work on Apple's products, was frowned upon by Jobs. Indeed, it drove a wedge between them for more than two decades. Although their companies remained intense rivals in several product categories, Bill and Steve, on May 30, 2007, appeared together on stage at the "D: All Things Digital" conference in Carlsbad, California. Steve's comment to a reporter for "USA Today" was, "It's not a big deal. I'm very fond of Bill. He and I have known each other longer than any two people in the industry. We used to be the youngest people in the room; now, we're the oldest."[1]

Indeed, the visionary Steve Jobs is no longer with us. He lost his battle with cancer on October 5, 2011 (shortly before this book went to press). He left us with many messages, not the least of which is: "Life can be much broader once you discover one simple fact, and that is, everything around you that you call life was made up by people that were no smarter than you ... the minute that you can understand that you can poke life ... that you can change it, you can mould it ... that's maybe the most important thing." (sic)

We Know Not Where We Go

I stated, on the first page of Part I, "What happened in our lives yesterday and what happens to us today prepares us for tomorrow." That statement will continue to ring true as long as we continue to learn and gain experience.

The lessons we have learned, especially those we have learned the hard way, and the skills we have independently developed do have a tendency to combine and will continue to combine, for us to conquer new challenges, previously unimaginable.

In a news article after his death, I read the following quote from Steve Jobs that echoes my statement above, but with much more clarity:

> Again, you can't connect the dots looking forward; you can only connect them looking backwards. So you have to trust that the dots will somehow connect in your future. You have to trust in something - your gut, destiny, life, karma, whatever. This approach has never let me down, and it has made all the difference in my life.
>
> --Steve Jobs

In my working life, and even in the years since retirement, my life has taken many twists and turns, and I have accomplished things I had never dreamed of. God willing, I have not yet finished my tiny contribution to mankind. Neither, I hope, have you.

---

1   USA Today, p. 1B, May 31, 2007

Glossary

A

ASSEMBLER

An assembler is a program that converts written instructions into a pattern of bits that will direct the computer's processor to perform the intended basic operations. Some people call these instructions assembler language and others use the term assembly language.

Most computers come with a specified set of very basic instructions that correspond to the basic machine operations that the computer can perform. The programmer can write a program using a sequence of these assembler instructions (source code).

When the assembler program is started, it takes each statement in the source code and generates a corresponding bit stream or pattern (a series of 0's and 1's of a given length).

The output of the assembler program is called the object code or object program. The sequence of 0's and 1's that constitute the object program is sometimes called machine code. The object program can then be run (executed) whenever desired without going through the process again.

In the earliest computers, programmers actually wrote programs in machine code, but assembler languages or instruction sets were soon developed to speed up programming. Today, assembler programming is used only where very efficient control over processor operations is needed. It requires knowledge of a particular computer's instruction set. Historically, most programs have been written in "higher-level" languages such as COBOL, FORTRAN, PL/I, and C. These languages are easier to learn and faster to write programs with than assembler language. The program that processes the source code written in these languages is called a compiler. Like the assembler, a compiler takes higher-level language statements and reduces them to machine code.

The assembler carries out some or all of the following functions:
- Translation of symbolic operation codes;
- Allocations of storage;
- Computation of absolute or relocatable addresses from symbolic addresses;
- Generation of sequences of symbolic instructions by the insertion of parameters supplied for each case into macro definitions;
- Insertion of library routines;

An assembler differs from a compiler chiefly in that it evaluates each symbolic instruction as though it stood alone or in the immediate context of a few preceding instructions. In general, there is a one-to-one correspondence between the symbolic instructions written by the programmer and machine instructions produced by the assembler.

B

BINARY NUMBER SYSTEM

A system of numbers which uses the base 2, and the digits 0 and 1. See NUMBER SYSTEM for basics. As an example, to determine the decimal value of the binary integer 11111000, the low-order digit represents its value (0) times 2^0 or 0 times 1, or 0_{10}. The second digit (0) times 2^1 represents 0_{10}, the third digit (0) times 2^2 represents 0_{10}. The fourth digit (1) times 2^3 represents 8_{10}. The fifth digit (1) times 2^4 represents 16_{10}. The sixth digit (1) times 2^5 represents 32_{10}. The seventh digit (1) times 2^6 represents 64_{10}. The eighth digit (1) times 2^7 represents 128_{10}. The sum of those $= 248_{10}$.

BIT

One binary digit, either a 0 or a 1.

BOOLEAN

Dealing with operations defined by Boolean Algebra, described by George Boole in 1854. It is the algebra of logical relationships.

Boolean logic is used for circuit design. One binary digit can have the value 0 or 1, representing the two different states of one bit in a digital circuit, typically high and low voltage. Circuits are like mathematical expressions containing variables; two expressions are equal for all values of the variables if the corresponding circuits have the same input-output behavior. Every possible input-output behavior can be modeled by a suitable Boolean expression.

Basic logic gates such as AND, OR, and NOT gates may be used alone, or in conjunction with other gates, to control digital electronics and circuitry. Whether these gates are wired in series or parallel controls the precedence of the operations.

BOOT, BOOT UP, or IPL

Literally, to raise oneself up from the bootstraps. In computer terms, to read and give control to a few initial instructions which are programmed to load other executable code, such as an operating system. Also known as Initial Program Load (IPL).

BPI

Bits per inch, a unit of measure of density, stating how many rows of continuous data bits can fit on an inch of magnetic tape.

BUFFER

An area of random access memory used as a temporary holding area for data, either while being read into the area, or written from the area.

BUG

Erroneous code in a program which causes the program to malfunction. The term has been in use with mechanical equipment for over a century. It is said to have been first applied to computers in 1945, when a moth was smashed between the contacts of a relay in the Mark II computer, and caused it to malfunction. In programming, bugs are usually due to human errors, even though we try to create perfect code. Indeed, performing the testing phase for a new or modified program is known as debugging.

BUS

A set of parallel electrical conductors, which each transfer one binary bit of a unit of data simultaneously. An 8-bit bus has 8 data conductors and can transfer 8 bits at a time. A 32-bit bus has 32 conductors and can transfer 32 bits at a time.

BYTE

A computer's equivalent of a human bite. A group of binary digits that are processed as one unit in a computer. In the S/360 a byte is composed of 8 binary bits. Each EBCDIC character is a byte, but a byte can also be part of something larger such as an instruction, or a binary number—for example, an integer or floating-point number.

C

CATHODE RAY TUBE (CRT)

A vacuum tube, such as or similar to, a television picture tube or a video terminal, used for displaying selected images or data. On some very early computers, CRTs were used as storage devices and were known as electrostatic storage tubes.

CD

Compact Disk, an optical disk on which sound or data is recorded in a digital binary format.

CENTRAL PROCESSING UNIT (CPU)

The basic unit of the computer which accomplishes all of the arithmetic, logical, and primary control functions of the system.

CHARACTER

An alphabetic character, numeric digit, punctuation mark or other symbol by which humans communicate. In a computer, the binary representation of such a symbol. Depending upon various standards, the computer representations of characters were or are either 6, 7, or 8 binary bits in length.

CHECKSUM

A checksum or hash sum is a fixed-size datum computed from an arbitrary block of digital data for the purpose of detecting accidental errors, especially during the transmission of that data. The integrity of the data can be checked at any later time by recomputing the checksum and comparing it with the stored one. If the checksums match, the data was almost certainly not altered (either intentionally or unintentionally).

COMPILER

A program for building programs. It produces a specific program for a particular problem by determining the author's intended meaning for each language statement—expressed according to defined language rules—then selecting or generating the instructions or subroutine linkages to accomplish the purpose gleaned from each such language statement, in turn.

A compiler processes statements written in a particular user-friendly programming language and turns them into machine language or "code" that a computer's processor uses.

The compiler first parses (or analyzes) all of the language statements syntactically, one after the other, and then, in one or more successive stages or "passes," builds the output code, making sure that statements that refer to other statements are referred to correctly in the final code. Traditionally, the output of the compilation has been called object code or sometimes an object module. (Note that the term "object" here is not related to object-oriented programming.) The object code is machine code that the processor will execute, one instruction at a time.

CORE MEMORY
See MAGNETIC CORE MEMORY

CPU
See CENTRAL PROCESSING UNIT.

CRT
See CATHODE RAY TUBE.

D

DECIMAL NUMBER SYSTEM

A system of numbers which uses the base 10, and the digits 0 to 9. See NUMBER SYSTEM for basics. As an example, for the decimal integer 248, the first digit to the left represents its value (8) times 10^0 or 8x1, or 8. The second digit (4) times 10^1 represents 40, the third digit (2) times 10^2 represents 200. The sum of those $= 248_{10}$.

For a less obvious calculation, see BINARY NUMBER SYSTEM.

DIP SWITCHES

A set of small on-off switches mounted inside computer hardware; used in place of jumpers to configure the machine for a user. Typically flipping one of the switches might toggle a single feature on or off.

DISK DRIVE

Either (1) a DISKETTE DRIVE, the hardware unit for writing and reading removable flexible diskettes, or (2) a corresponding unit which uses removable rigid disk packs, or (3) a HARD DISK, a corresponding unit using nonremovable disks. In this case the disk drive includes the disks.

DISKETTE

Also known as a floppy disk. A flexible round disk with a magnetic coating and a metal hub, all encased in a jacket with access holes through which magnetic heads can read or write a specified circular concentric track, when the disk is spinning at a prescribed speed. Early diskettes were 8 inches in diameter. Smaller diskettes—5¼-inch and 3½-inch—became very popular for use in personal computers.

DISKETTE DRIVE

A unit for writing and reading a removable diskette. Magnetic heads are mounted on sliding arms (often called actuators) which position a given head for reading or writing concentric tracks when the disk is spinning at a prescribed speed.

DOT MATRIX

A type of printer that forms characters and other forms on paper by repeatedly striking selected pins, through an inked ribbon, against the paper as it forms each line. Early models used 9 pins, later increased to 24 pins for better resolution. They were widely used with early PCs.

E

EAM

Electric Accounting Machinery, predecessors to electronic computers, based on the processing of data in the form of punched cards. Limited programming was accomplished using pluggable wires in control panels.

F

FIXED POINT

A notation or system of arithmetic in which all numeric quantities are expressed by a predetermined number of digits and in which the point is implicitly located at some predetermined position. Contrast with floating point.

FLOATING POINT

In computing, floating point describes a system for representing real numbers which supports a wide range of values. Numbers are generally represented approximately to a fixed number of significant digits and scaled using an exponent. The base for the scaling is normally 2, 10 or 16. The typical number that can be represented is of the form:

$$\text{significant digits} \times \text{base}^{\text{exponent}}$$

Such a number is said to be normalized when the exponent is chosen so that the point is positioned immediately to the left of the most significant digit, to enhance accuracy.

FLOPPY DISK
See DISKETTE.

G

G

A metric system notation for Giga, or a billion. The accepted convention (not always observed) in computer applications is for upper case G to mean 2^{30}, or 1,073,741,824, and lower case g to mean 1,000,000,000. Example: 32G would mean 2^{35} or 34,359,738,368 whereas 32g would mean 32,000,000,000.

GIGO

"Garbage In, Garbage Out," a phrase stating that if input data is unreliable, the corresponding output data will be equally unreliable or worse.

GUI

Graphical User Interface. A means of displaying any desired graphics on a computer screen that is divided into a dense pattern—rows of dots called Picture Elements (PELs or Pixels), as on a television screen. One or more predetermined areas of the screen, often within designs called icons, may be selected to cause a preprogrammed action.

H

HARD DISK

A rigid set of nonremovable round disks with a magnetic coating and spaced on a rotating shaft. Magnetic heads are mounted on sliding arms (often called actuators) which position a given head for reading or writing concentric tracks when the disk is spinning at a prescribed speed.

HEXADECIMAL, "HEX" NUMBER SYSTEM

A system of numbers which uses the base 16 and 16 digits, 0 to 9 and A through F. See NUMBER SYSTEM for basics.

As an example, to determine the decimal value of the hex integer F8, the low-order digit represents its value (8) times 16^0 or 8 times 1, or 8_{10}. The second digit (F_{16}), or 15_{10} times 16^1 represents 240_{10}. The sum of those two decimal values = 248_{10}.

HOLLERITH CODE

Representations of letters, numbers, or special symbols punched into 80-column cards with 12 rows, each column containing a pattern of holes representing the character.

I

INTEGER

A number that has no nonzero fractional component, i.e. it is either the number 0 or an exact multiple of the number 1 or -1.

INTERPRETER

A program which, like an assembler or a compiler, translates each statement of a source program into machine code. Unlike assemblers and compilers at that point, rather than adding that machine code to an executable file (for later execution), it causes it to be executed immediately. The primary advantage of an interpreter is in the immediate execution of the object program. The main disadvantage, for a program to be executed many times, is that it will be run substantially slower than its equivalent executable file created by an assembler or a compiler.

IPL

Initial Program Load. To read and give control to a few initial instructions which are programmed to load other executable code, such as an operating system. Also known as a Boot.

J

JCL

Job Control Language, a term coined to depict statements written to control computer jobs under OS/360. A JCL statement would either be punched into an IBM card or recorded as an 80-character card image. One example of a JCL statement would invoke a desired program, and would specify the input and output parameters.

K

K

A metric system notation for Kilo, or 1000. The accepted convention (not always observed) in computer applications is for upper case K to mean 2^{10}, or 1024, and lower case k to mean 1000. Example: 32K would mean 2^{15} or 32,768 whereas 32k would mean 32,000.

L

LOWER CASE

Small letters a through z, as opposed to upper case (A through Z).

M

M

A metric system notation for Mega, or a million. The accepted convention (not always observed) in computer applications is for upper case M to mean 2^{20}, or 1,048,576, and lower case m to mean 1,000,000. Example: 32M would mean 2^{25} or 33,554,432 whereas 32m would mean 32,000,000.

MAGNETIC CORE MEMORY

A binary memory device in which information is represented by the magnetic polarities of many tiny permeable rings. Addressing is accomplished by wires running, in x and y directions through an array of such rings, each of which represents a binary bit. Sensing is performed by another set of wires running through the rings in a z direction.

MAGNETIC DISK
See DISKETTE

MAGNETIC DISK DRIVE
See DISK DRIVE, DISKETTE DRIVE, HARD DISK

MAINFRAME

Generally a large scale computer. A mainframe may do any or all of (1) run batch jobs, (2) interact with many terminals, (3) interact with satellite computers. It may be a server.

MERCURY DELAY TUBES

A computer memory based on the piezoelectric property of quartz crystals, one writing at one end of a tube of mercury and another crystal reading at the other end.

MINICOMPUTER, "MINI"

A medium sized digital computer which could be shared by several users from terminals, or which could be used for a single task at a much lower cost than a large computer. Digital Equipment Corporation (DEC) is believed to have been the first to put the concept of minicomputers into practice with its PDP series in the early 1960s.

MIT
Massachusetts Institute of Technology.

MODEM
A contraction of modulator-demodulator. By modulating the digital signals from a computer onto high frequency waves, called a carrier, data can be sent from a computer over an ordinary phone line. At the receiving end the signal is demodulated, separating the data from the carrier, and stored in the processor's memory.

MULTIPROGRAMMING
The process of running several programs concurrently in a computer. By interleaving their access efficiently, it appears to the user of each program that theirs has exclusive use of the computer.

MULTITASKING
See MULTIPROGRAMMING.

N

NUMBER SYSTEM
Number theory specifies rules for number systems in general. A number system has a base, or radix, assumed or indicated by a subscript following the number (e.g. 248_{10} for a decimal number) and digits from 0 up to the base minus 1.

For an integer, each digit, progressing from the lowest-order digit, represents a value times a progressively higher power of the base, starting with the base to the zero power (which is always 1). See BINARY NUMBER SYSTEM, DECIMAL NUMBER SYSTEM, HEXADECIMAL NUMBER SYSTEM, and OCTAL NUMBER SYSTEM for examples. The subscripted base number is always shown as a decimal value. Decimal, octal, and binary equivalents of hexadecimal digits are as follows:

Hex digit	Decimal	Octal	Binary
0	0	0	0
1	1	1	1
2	2	2	10
3	3	3	11
4	4	4	100
5	5	5	101
6	6	6	110
7	7	7	111
8	8	10	1000
9	9	11	1001
A	10	12	1010
B	11	13	1011
C	12	14	1100
D	13	15	1101
E	14	16	1110
F	15	17	1111

OCTAL NUMBER SYSTEM

A number system based on the radix 8, and using the digits 0 to 7. See NUMBER SYSTEM for basics.

As an example, to determine the decimal value of the octal integer 370_8, the low-order digit represents its value (0) times 8^0 or 0 times 1, or 0_{10}. The second digit (7_8), or 7_{10} times 8^1 represents 56_{10}. The third digit (3_8), or 3_{10} times 8^2 represents 192_{10}. The sum of those three decimal values = 248_{10}.

ONLINE

In the early days of computing, this meant having immediate access to a computer, generally via a terminal linked to a teleprocessing program. On-line operations are generally classified as foreground, as contrasted with batch operations which are run in the background at lower priority for CPU cycles. Now when people talk about being online, they mean being operational or being connected to the internet.

P

PC

Personal Computer. The term was applied by IBM to a microcomputer it announced in 1981. Since then, the term PC has been generically applied by many to microcomputers in general.

PEL (PIXEL)

Picture Element or Pixel. On a video graphics screen, each dot in many rows of dots is called a PEL. By design, PELs are so close together that our eyes do not see the individual dots, but rather the picture they form.

PROGRAM (noun)

A set of computer instructions that perform a defined function. The collection of statements to be assembled, compiled, or interpreted is called a Source Program. The machine code produced from a Source Program by an assembler or compiler is called an Object Program.

PROGRAM (verb)

To create statements which, together, will produce a computer program when translated into computer instructions. The language used in the statements is defined according to the compiler, assembler, or interpreter which will make the translation.

R

RAM

Random Access Memory, a storage medium in which each addressable unit is directly accessible. RAM generally implies memory that is both readable and writable, i.e. excluding Read Only Memory (ROM).

RAMAC

Random Access Method of Accounting and Control–the first computer with a hard disk. Introduced by IBM in 1956, it was half computer and half tabulator. It used drum memory for storage.

RANDOM ACCESS

That property of a memory device whereby each addressable unit (such as a byte) within that device is directly accessible, i.e. each addressed unit of storage may be directly accessed independently of other units.

REGISTER

Registers are storage areas inside the processor where the information can be accessed very quickly. Information can be loaded into registers, manipulated or tested in some way (using machine instructions for arithmetic/logic/comparison) and then used as a basis for program action, decision-making, output, or stored back into memory, possibly at a different location. When a program is debugged, register contents may be analyzed to determine the computer's status at the time of failure.

Address registers are special registers to store and manipulate addresses. In the early days of computing, the programmers had to keep track of the memory space they were using and directly assign it to special functions.

The Base register would hold the "starting" address and address registers would usually hold the displacement from that address.

ROM

Read Only Memory. Randomly accessed memory which is prewritten (by the manufacturer) and can be read but not changed (cannot be rewritten).

S

SCRATCH TAPE
Like a scratch pad for computers, a scratch tape is a magnetic tape that is used to store temporary data that can be erased. The tape is then reused for other data or applications.

SERIAL
The property of a transmission medium whereby bits are moved in series, or one at a time. Serial is the opposite of parallel, whereby multiple bits are moved simultaneously, by means of multiple electrical conductors.

SERVER
A computer that communicates with, or serves, other computers. Servers are to be found managing networks of any number of computers. One of a server's tasks is to recognize all the nodes in its network and direct transmissions to the appropriate node.

T

T
A metric system notation for Tera, or a trillion. The accepted convention (not always observed) in computer applications is for upper case T to mean 2^{40}, or 1,099,511,627,776, and lower case t to mean 1,000,000,000,000. Example: 32T would mean 2^{45} or 35,184,372,088,832 whereas 32t would mean 32,000,000,000,000.

TP or TP TERMINAL
Teleprocessing terminal (TP terminal) connected to the mainframe.

TSO

Time Sharing Option (TSO) took the place of TSS, and was eventually replaced by running under Virtual Machine. TSO operated in batch or interactively. Interactive users operated in either a line-by-line mode or in a full screen, menu-driven mode. In the line-by-line mode, the user enters commands by typing them in at the keyboard; in turn, the system interprets the commands, and then displays responses on the terminal screen.

TSS

Time Sharing System (TSS) was an expensive failure that the technology could not adequately support. TSS/360 failed primarily due to performance and reliability problems, and lack of compatibility with OS/360, although those issues were eventually addressed.

Time-sharing developed out of the realization that while any single user was inefficient, a large group of users together were not. This was due to the pattern of interaction; in most cases users entered bursts of information followed by long pause, but a group of users working at the same time would mean that the pauses of one user would be used up by the activity of the others. Given an optimal group size, the overall process could be very efficient. Similarly, small slices of time spent waiting for disk, tape, or network input could be granted to other users.

U

UPPER CASE

Capital letters A through Z, as opposed to lower case (a through z).

V

VIRTUAL STORAGE

An apparently larger primary computer memory than is real. The illusion is made possible by algorithms by which secondary memory supplements primary memory, transparently to the user.

W

WILLIAMS TUBES

The Williams tube or the Williams-Kilburn tube (after inventors Freddie Williams and Tom Kilburn), developed in about 1946 or 1947, was a cathode ray tube used to electronically store binary data. Each Williams tube could store roughly 512–1024 bits of data. It was the first random-access digital storage device, and was used successfully in several early computers.

WORD

A word is a unit of data of a defined bit length that can be addressed and moved between storage and the computer processor. Usually, the defined bit length of a word is equivalent to the width of the computer's data bus so that a word can be moved in a single operation from storage to a processor register. For any computer architecture with an eight-bit byte, the word will be some multiple of eight bits. In IBM's evolutionary System/360 architecture, a word is 32 bits, or four contiguous eight-bit bytes. In Intel's PC processor architecture, a word is 16 bits, or two contiguous eight-bit bytes.

A word can contain a computer instruction, a storage address, or application data that is to be manipulated in some way. In general, the longer the architected word length, the more the computer processor can do in a single operation.

Resources

Following are some publications to which I am indebted:

Blue Magic; The People, Power and Politics Behind the IBM Personal Computer, James Chposky and Ted Leonsis, 1988

"Concept of Digital Computer Didn't Come Easily: John V. Atanasoff, DP Pioneer—Part II," *Computerworld*, March 1974

Glossary of Programming and Computing Terms, (unclassified) Pacific Missile Range, D.E. Denk and J.S. Holmes, 1960, 1962, ASTIA

IBM 7090 Data Processing System, Reference Manual, IBM, 1961

IBM 7094 Data Processing System, Reference Manual, IBM, 1962

IBM 7094 Principles of Operation, IBM, 1962

Microsoft Secrets; How the World's Most Powerful Software Company Creates Technology, Shapes Markets, and Manages People, Michael A. Cusumano and Richard W. Selby, 1995

The Computer Pioneers, David Ritchie, 1986

The Macintosh Way, Guy Kawasaki, 1990

West of Eden: The End of Innocence at Apple Computer, Frank Rose, 1989

Index

D

E

F

J

K

L

M

T